# Your Vizsla

By John X. Strauz and
Joseph F. Cunningham

*Compiled and Edited by*

William W. Denlinger and R. Annabel Rathman

**DENLINGER'S**

Fairfax, Virginia 22030

Reproduced on the front cover is a pastel portrait of Ch. Puerco Pete Barat by Robert C. Hickey, the famous animal artist. (Photograph courtesy Tim Ennis.) Pictured on the back cover is Dual Ch. Weedy Creek Lobo, owned by Harold R. Wingerter, Muscatine, Iowa.

International Standard Book Number: 0-87714-006-5

Library of Congress Catalog Card Number: 70-187775

Judge Joseph F. Cunningham awards Best of Breed to Ch. Gold-N-Rust Dare-devil, U.D., handled by Jane Forsyth, at the Staten Island Kennel Club Show, 1971. Steward is John X. Strauz.

# Foreword

The United States, a democracy, is a curious guardian of an historic object of royal sovereignty. The oldest part of the crown consists of two bands of gold topped by a cross. This part was sent to Stephen I of Hungary (977-1038) by Pope Sylvester when he bestowed the title "Apostolic King" upon him. The lower broad band of gold was a gift from the Byzantine Emperor Michael Lukas to King Geza I. This is the Holy Crown of Hungary, not only a national symbol, but also part of the Magyar Mystique. The Magyars attributed the powers of sovereignty to the Holy Crown itself.

Before and during World War II, the crown was kept under constant guard by the Magyar Vizsla, the national sporting dog of Hungary. The Vizsla is also part of the Magyar Mystique. The Vizsla as a recognizable breed is as old as the crown and as such is the world's first sporting breed. The Holy Crown and the Vizsla are integral parts of the mosaic of historic pageantry of the Magyars.

We are humbly grateful to four Hungarian sportsmen for providing us with some of the historic material on the breed through correspondence with us and through publication of their research in the "Vizsla News," official publication of the Vizsla Club of America: the late Count Bela Hadik of Chester, New Hampshire; the late Baron Mihaly Kende of Budapest; the late Colonel Jeno Dus of Hamburg, New York; and Dr. Bill Kemenes-Kettner of Canada.

And last but most important to us personally, we dedicate this book to the dean of American dog show judges, Alva Rosenberg, who gave us encouragement and support after the breed was recognized in 1960 by The American Kennel Club.

John X. Strauz and Joseph F. Cunningham

# Contents

An aggressive young puppy which grew up to be Ch. Glen Cottage D'Hadur, owned by Joseph Burkhardt.

Ch. Glen Cottage Diva with a litter of twelve puppies sired by Ch. Puerco Pete Barat.

## Selecting Your Vizsla Puppy

People who buy purebred dogs do so for one main reason: they are buying a kind of dog whose nature and type are already known to them through other specimens. Occasionally in one of the rarer breeds, such as the Vizsla, the purchaser is anxious to buy the unknown and exotic in order to play a sort of social "oneupmanship." This is a pitfall for both the buyer and the breeder and not infrequently results in a puppy's being returned. The Vizsla which starts out as a spoiled novelty puppy turns out to be a too-demanding responsibility. We know of at least one household where divorce was the answer to the divided opinion over the Vizsla. Often the puppy is returned because the buyer does not know the breed and its demonstrative nature. Another more commonly known breed might fit the buyer's need more closely.

You would hardly expect your authors, Vizsla breeders themselves, to recommend purchasing puppies from anyone but a seasoned, reputable breeder. As serious breeders, we have learned to examine the prospective purchaser's needs and desires and mode of living just as scrupulously as he examines our puppies and breeding stock.

This part of the negotiation is more important than any other. If the breeder finds that both husband and wife are employed and that there is no one to be left with the puppy, the breeder must refuse to sell them a puppy. A young puppy left alone will howl and chew until the owners bring him back to the breeder within the week. A puppy must be "humanized" while being weaned (generally at six to eight weeks of age) and immediately afterward, to make him more receptive to his master's wants. In order to accomplish this, humans must be with the puppy a good part of the day.

No matter what your purpose is in selecting a Vizsla—pet, show, or field, or as is often the case, all three—you should select a lively, aggressive puppy that stands out from the herd of litter mates. There are often a dozen puppies in a litter, so care is needed in evaluating them. A reliable breeder will tell you the truth about the quality of the puppy and whether it is pet quality or show stock.

The reputable breeder will tell you the truth because, first of all, he is not swayed by financial considerations. This may sound strange to the uninitiated, but the serious breeder of purebred dogs is breeding for the love of his breed, only. Breeding quality dogs is an expensive avocation and a very handsome salary is necessary to the breeder of successful show and field dogs.

If the breeder wants to perpetuate his bloodlines, he must place his puppies selectively. The pet puppy sales must be made to good homes where the Vizsla temperament can be nurtured and developed to its fullest. These pet Vizslas, in themselves, create a demand for similar specimens. Every breeder has an excess of pet stock that eat just as much as blue ribbon winners. This is why you can expect to pay a lower price for the pet quality puppy. A serious breeder will always try to hold onto the pick of the litter dog and bitch himself, especially if he is show oriented. And every successful breeder today must be show oriented. So hold onto your hat when he quotes prices on these, for he is going to make you "pay through the nose" for taking his *best puppies* away.

The most successful transactions are those in which both buyer and breeder are perfectly frank with each other. If you, as buyer, state honestly that you are looking for a show specimen, the breeder will make every effort to select the best possible puppy, for you will take a great financial responsibility from the breeder's shoulders by showing his good product at your own expense.

A word of caution to the newcomer to the dog-show game: don't be blinded by the name of a top-winning dog or bitch on the basis of his own wins alone. Some of the greatest winners are not the best producers and do not pass their own outstanding qualities on to their puppies. Your best chance to select a winning show dog is to make your purchase from a kennel with a few generations of champions and winners—even though the kennel breeds on a modest scale. In this case your puppy is backed by proven winning bloodlines, rather than by an isolated winner from an average background. This is the type of breeder who is striving to produce the best Vizsla possible, and in order to confirm his breeding skills and his judgment, he finishes all the conformation ring and field trial champions he can in each generation.

The best way to buy a good Vizsla puppy is the way you would buy anything else: shop around and compare. A reputable and successful breeder knows you will come back to him after looking elsewhere, so he can spend the time with you even if you tell him you are going to visit another breeder. Do not be misled by the breeder who claims his dogs and puppies have no faults. The perfect dog has yet to be bred.

In selecting your Vizsla puppy, make sure that the dewclaws have been removed and the tail docked to the correct length. Ideally, dewclaws are removed three days to one week after whelping. Postponing it to a much later time involves more elaborate surgical procedures utilizing anesthesia. The removal of the dewclaws, both front and rear, should be done by a veterinarian, who will decide if stitches are required.

During this same visit to the veterinarian, the tail should be docked one-third off. It is in docking that most novice breeders go wrong in advising their veterinarian on the correct length. Because of the relative rarity of the Vizsla, the average veterinarian cannot be expected to know the correct tail length. The most common mistake the novice Vizsla breeder makes in docking is to advise one-third left on, the opposite of what the Standard calls for.

We do not dock by measuring the tail in total and automatically indicate the dock at the top third. Rather, we consider the size of the puppy, his squareness or longness when viewed in total profile, and select his tail length somewhere about the end third where it seems proper for him. A proper dock should leave a gently curving arch to the tail. The tail is left longer than that of the Weimaraner or German Shorthaired Pointer.

Because we wean our puppies early, they are ready to go to owners at six weeks of age. At this age the puppy's eye color is still in the final stage of transition from blue to brown. The best clue is to examine the eye color of the sire and dam. If both have the favored dark brown eyes, matching the darkest part of their coat color, the puppies should carry this same eye color. If one parent has dark eyes and the other light or near-yellow, which is objectionable, the mature eye color of the puppy is open to conjecture.

Pigmentation of the nose and pads of the six-week-old is the same as it was at birth and will be into maturity—a flesh-colored or pinkish suntan brown similar to the coat color. At six weeks the puppy coat is slightly lighter than it will be at maturity, but not appreciably so. A light colored puppy will not mature to the desirable rich red cast. If the puppy doesn't have a darker saddle at six weeks of age, he never will.

The six-week-old puppy is basically a miniature of what he will be as a mature dog. If his body length and leg length are square and compact, he will maintain this proportion into maturity. If he is a bit long in the back or leg, he will grow up with these less-than-ideal characteristics. In selecting a Vizsla, it is best not to decide on the

Keith Piechoki, with his newly acquired puppy out of "Maggie" (owned by Art and Theresa Lattimer) and sired by Ch. Glen Cottage Fred Barbaroosa (owned by the authors).

biggest or the smallest puppy in the litter unless it is acquired for pet purposes exclusively. This is advised because of the wide variation in Vizsla size three and four generations back, when dogs weighed from thirty-five to eighty pounds at maturity. Litters often include throwbacks to either extreme—depending on the particular bloodlines.

In judging the head of a young Vizsla puppy, look for a tight eye covering, especially a tight lower lid. The muzzle in profile should be more square at the nose than tapered. The puppy at this age often has a rather domed skull with a prominent occipital projection at the top and back of his head but will develop a flatter head with a rounded skull at the rear tied into a nicely arched neck.

Above all, young puppies should be exuberant and playful and healthy looking. They should look well fed and a bit fat at the stomach, but not rotund or puffy. They will still be a bit gangly and awkward on their feet. There is no way to judge their gaiting ability at this age, but at maturity they will reflect their parents in this respect.

Do not be afraid to purchase your Vizsla from a kennel many hundreds of miles away. As a matter of fact, you will probably have to, because there are not many breeders of Vizslas. If you communicate your wants objectively and honestly through correspondence with the breeder, you can secure exactly the type of puppy to fit your needs. Puppies are shipped by air with the new owner paying the shipping costs.

When buying a puppy sight unseen, it is very important to select a breeder of sound reputation. The regional Vizsla club of your state will assist you in contacting the Vizsla breeders in your area. If a recommended Vizsla breeder does not have any puppies available, he will be happy to suggest the name of another breeder who does. In fact, it is the business of a good breeder to be aware of the breedings of other successful Vizsla kennels.

The purchaser of a puppy should receive from the breeder either the individual application from the A.K.C. litter registration, or an individual registration certificate if the dog has already been named and has been registered by the A.K.C. The buyer should also expect to receive a four- to six-generation pedigree for the puppy and the puppy's medical history and immunization record. The puppy should already have received distemper, hepatitis, and leptospirosis shots. If he is to be shipped across state boundaries, he should also have had a rabies shot.

11

Ch. Bok Selle Son of a Gun, winner of the 1966 National Specialty of the Vizsla Club of America. Owners, Dr. and Mrs. Maynard Wolfe, Montclair, New Jersey.

# The Adult Vizsla

The American Vizsla Standard was developed by the Vizsla Club of America and adopted by The American Kennel Club as official when that governing body recognized the breed in December 1960.

## The Standard for the Vizsla

*General appearance*—that of a medium sized dog of quite distinguished appearance. Robust but rather lightly built, his short coat is an attractive rusty-gold, and his tail is docked. He is a dog of power and drive in the field, and a tractable and affectionate companion in the home.

*Head*—lean but muscular. The skull is moderately wide between the ears, with a median line down the forehead. Stop moderate. The muzzle is a trifle longer than the skull and, although tapering, is well squared at its end. Jaws strong, with well-developed white teeth meeting in a scissors bite. The lips cover the jaws completely but they are neither loose nor pendulous. Nostrils slightly open, the nose brown. A black or slate gray nose is objectionable. Ears—thin, silky and proportionately long, with rounded-leather ends; set fairly low and hanging close to the cheeks. Eyes—medium in size and depth of setting, their surrounding tissue covering the whites, and the iris or color portion harmonizing with the shade of coat. A yellow eye is objectionable.

*Neck*—strong, smooth, and muscular; moderately long, arched and devoid of dewlap. It broadens nicely into shoulders which are well laid back.

*Body*—strong and well proportioned. The back is short, the withers high, and the topline slightly rounded over the loin to the set-on of the tail. Chest moderately broad and deep, and reaching down to the elbows. Ribs well sprung and underline exhibiting a slight tuck-up beneath the loin.

*Legs and feet*—forelegs straight, strong and muscular, with elbows close. The hind legs have well-developed thighs, with moderate angulation at stifles and hocks. Too much angulation at the hocks is as faulty as too little. The hocks, which are well let down, are equidistant from each other from the hock joint to the ground. Cowhocks are faulty. Feet are cat-like, round and compact, with toes close. Nails are brown and short; pads thick and tough. Dewclaws, if any, to be removed. Hare feet are objectionable.

*Tail*—set just below the level of the back, thicker at the root, and docked one-third off.

*Coat*—short, smooth, dense, and close-lying, without woolly undercoat.

*Color*—solid. Rusty gold or rather dark sandy yellow in different shades, with darker shades preferred. Dark brown and pale yellow are undesirable. Small white spots on chest or feet are not faulted.

*Temperament*—that of a natural hunter endowed with a good nose and above average ability to take training. Lively, gentle mannered, and demonstratively affectionate. Fearless and with well-developed protective instinct.

*Gait*—far reaching, light footed, graceful, smooth.

*Size*—dogs, 22 to 24 inches shoulder height; 45 to 60 lbs. weight; bitches, 21 to 23 inches shoulder height; 40 to 55 lbs. Oversize not to be considered a major fault unless excessive.

13

International judge and author of *The New German Shorthaired Pointer,* Mrs. C. Bede Maxwell, demonstrating the gait of Ch. Puerco Pete Barat. Mrs. Maxwell says of this photograph, "It is the only picture I have seen of a sporting dog gaiting taken from that front-end angle and showing such magnificent coordination . . . you should draw very definite attention . . . to the demonstrated front action and the thrust of the hind action."

The Standard was further modified in January 1964 after many serious breeders in the Vizsla Club of America became concerned about the excessive size in the breed. Twenty-six and twenty-seven inch dogs were becoming common and were winning at the dog shows. As chairman of the Standards Committee of the National Club, one of your authors spearheaded the drive among the membership and made the motion to limit the size of the Vizsla. The motion carried and The American Kennel Club concurred. The Vizsla Club of America is to be congratulated on its purposefulness—which is especially commendable in a relatively new club. Many other sporting breed clubs are still wrangling with the problem and breeding has probably gone too far in divergent directions to reach a unanimity of opinion.

The modification of the Vizsla Standard was published in the January 1964 issue of "Pure Bred Dogs—American Kennel Gazette":

*Size*—males 22 to 24 inches, females 21 to 23 inches at the highest point of the shoulders. Any dog measuring over or under these limits shall be considered faulty, the seriousness of the fault depending on the extent of the deviation. Any dog that measures more than 2 inches over or under these limits shall be disqualified.

The breed Standard is really very brief and as such can give only a limited impression of the variations possible within it. A long acquaintance with the breed is necessary to define the finer points of beauty in the breed. Tail length and coat color have been two of the most debated features in the breed up to the present time. Coat color in America originally came in two predominant shades— a light sandy yellow-tan and a deep red, almost as dark as the coat of the Irish Setter. The lighter colored coat generally was found on large, big-boned dogs, while the darker color seemed to be seen more often on the smaller, more compact dogs. This difference gave rise to the belief that there was more than one type of Vizsla in Hungary. A more exacting interpretation would be that the different bloodlines in Hungary seemed to carry their own characteristics.

As we go into the second decade of recognition by the A.K.C., breeders from both coasts and the Midwest have had the opportunity to study each other's dogs at our national specialty shows and field trials. The inevitable has happened in that dogs from all over the United States and Canada have been interbred. The darker reddish color seems to be dominant, for the majority of the breed now carry this coat.

Some of the finest specimens in the breed carry the "Esterhazy saddle," or stripe, as it is known in Hungary today. A neighbor

15

Wirehaired Vizslas (courtesy of Carole Smith, Editor, "The Vizsla News").

Vikingsholm Ingaar as portrayed by Ole Larson. One of a series of breed portraits commissioned by Parke, Davis and Company, and reproduced courtesy that company.

of ours, Dr. Elizabeth Jones Lukacs, a Kuvasz breeder who assisted in judging at the Budapest show in the spring of 1971, observed that all the Vizslas at that show were darkish red and had the saddle marking. The saddle is a darker shading of the coat color over the back. The darker shading slopes downwards over the shoulder and from there it narrows and goes back to the tail where it becomes the tail color or is a darker stripe on the top surface of the tail. The shape of the shaded area is, in fact, that of an English riding saddle with an elongated back portion.

Tail length was once a serious problem because the breeders and veterinarians did not check the Standard's "one-third off" stipulation. Tails are now uniform, with the gently curving arch upward, so necessary for seeing the dog in the field in tall grass.

The darker coated dogs have a darker eye that is very handsome and conforms to coat color. A yellow eye is objectionable, but your authors have observed only one specimen with yellow eyes.

Although the Standard calls the Vizsla nose "brown," a more accurate description might be pinkish tan. The late Count Bela Hadik called it "flesh" color. We will agree with his description if the flesh is given a suntan.

The statement in the Vizsla Standard which reads, "The muzzle is a trifle longer than the skull . . ." is incorrect. Actually, the reverse is true, for the skull of the Vizsla is and always has been longer than the muzzle. The Vizsla Club of America has under consideration a proposed change in the Standard which will correct this erroneous statement.

The wirehaired Hungarian Vizsla is a separate breed developed from the Vizsla and the Wirehaired German Pointer in the 1930s by Joseph Vanna. It is very popular in the rugged northern part of Hungary and Slovakia. The Standard is the same for the Wirehaired Vizsla except for the coat. This Vizsla has short, coarse hair on his face and has a short beard. He is completely covered with a rough, wirehaired coat. This breed is not recognized by The American Kennel Club and we do not believe any specimens are in the United States.

The American, Canadian, and Hungarian Standards for the Vizsla are all very much alike in wording and content. There are minor differences, of course, but none which will keep the breeding of the Vizsla restricted to a particular country.

Pamela Hope Winters, age two and one-half years, and her constant companion, Ch. Glen Cottage Charlie, age three. Photograph by E. Cahail.

Nina, a fine bitch living in Barryville, New York, watching television.

## Vizsla Personality

It is very difficult to describe the magnificent personality of the Vizsla without being carried away by the use of superlatives. We will start with the generally accepted facts first and develop our theme later.

The Vizsla is a good natured, tractable dog which takes to training very easily. He trains easily because of the dominant characteristic of the breed—he wishes to please. He is very clean in his habits—almost cat-like in this respect, licking his paws and coat. He preens himself. He sheds very little if he receives a good brushing occasionally.

The Vizsla is said by the official Standard to be aristocratic in his bearing, and he does look aristocratic. But the word "aristocratic" implies disdain and might more perfectly describe the somewhat aloof Afghan Hound. "Aristocratic clown" might be a more apt description of the Vizsla's nature, though not of his looks.

In the first chapter of this book we mentioned "humanizing" your puppy. This is particularly important with the Vizsla. By constant association with his master and the family, the Vizsla matures into an animal of great love and response, which, in depth of feeling, cannot be compared easily to any other breed. Basically, the Vizsla is all dog and is intelligent as a dog should be, not as a human is. There is nothing cute about him except when he is a very young puppy, and he loses this appeal quickly as he grows to be a dog. Sometimes the Vizsla acts as though he thinks he is a monkey or a cat, but basically he is right at the top of the list as man's oldest companion.

The Vizsla is a very intelligent animal, as is befitting to a good bird dog. He responds to obedience training very quickly because of his intelligence, which also tells him how to please his master. Vizslas were entered in obedience trials long before they were permitted in the show ring in the United States. It is "duck soup" for a Vizsla to acquire his Companion Dog title at nine months of age. Because of his superior intelligence, the adult Vizsla will try to get more than his due unless the family stops him. Vizslas don't sit on the floor when there is a vacant upholstered chair to sit on. Vizslas don't sleep on mats or on expensive wicker beds. They sleep on their owner's bed and some have to sleep under the covers on chilly nights. Since the Vizsla is exceptionally clean, we will let the reader work out his own solution.

The Vizsla is extremely sensitive in his reactions to his family's emotions. If a child cries, he is right there to comfort it. If someone he loves lets out a real belly laugh, he will be transfixed with joy, making Vizsla noises and dancing around on his hind legs.

The Hungarians learned in the twenties that persuasion was the key to training the breed, not roughness, even for the stiffest field competition. The Vizsla's sensitive intelligence is to be appealed to in training him. Paul Sabo, one of the top field trainers in the country, considers the Vizsla to be generally higher strung than the other pointing breeds, and this factor should be taken into account by the handler-owner when working Vizslas or preparing them to run at a formal trial. Training a Vizsla is roughly comparable to training a thoroughbred colt. Kindness is the key in the success of training either. However, we do not mean to imply that the Vizsla is as skittish as the colt. Vizslas need a lot of "talking to" but not "yelling at." The latter will only confuse him and "burn" you.

We do not mean to imply that a good rap on the rump isn't in order when you need to chastise him. He is still a dog, and he knows it even though he doesn't always act as if he remembers.

Throughout the ages, the Vizsla has been called fearless, which may seem a little incongruous considering his sensitivity. However, if the mature Vizsla has been raised with loving kindness, he develops a sort of superegotism which does not leave room for any such base emotion as fear. Hubert Will, an outstanding animal trainer, works his Vizslas right along with leopards. Will says that the Vizslas taught the leopard kitten who was boss when the kitten weighed eight pounds, and even though the leopard now weighs over a hundred pounds, the Vizsla still has his original opinion of the cat.

The non-biting characteristic of the Vizsla is important for the novice Vizsla owner to know, because the Vizsla does have another habit which could be misconstrued as biting. In fact, this happened to us with a prospective puppy buyer.

The Vizsla, as a good bird dog, is fond of retrieving birds, chewing on pine cones, and as a puppy, chewing anything he can get his mouth around. He has a soft mouth, and is very "orally" oriented, to borrow the psychologist's phrase. If your Vizsla is in a happy mood, walking along with you, he may just take your whole hand in his mouth and prance right along at your side, pleased as he can be.

Ch. Glen Cottage Adam, owned by Joan Marie Smith.

As a puppy and youngster, he will nibble on fingers, but softly, never drawing blood.

The prospective buyer we mentioned earlier had picked out his puppy and we had moved into the house to finalize negotiations. One of our older house dogs got playful and took the buyer's hand in his mouth. The no-longer-prospective buyer leaped out of his chair and claimed he was bitten. He yelled that he did not want a vicious dog. We mumbled something to the effect that we were pleased that he was not hurt, and sighed with relief as he and his wife went off to check on another breed.

The only difficulty with this playful habit occurs when you are trying to lead-train Vizsla puppies. They tend to want to hold the lead in their mouth while prancing around. This looks very cute, for they are extremely pleased with themselves for knowing what lead-training is all about. However, this is not quite what the show judge has in mind when gaiting a dog.

The Vizsla is too much dog for some people because he demands so much attention. If you want an "old dog Ruff," who lies on the back porch all day—forget the Vizsla. The Vizsla fully expects to share equally in everything the family does. In case you have not gathered by now—he is a housedog, and has been for centuries. He has never been put out to the barn or stable with the rest of the hunting dogs.

Your sensitive Vizsla will not mature to full intelligence and affection if he is kenneled or locked away from the family. This same sensitivity works both ways: Vizslas don't run away from home or get lost—it wouldn't occur to them to leave those they love.

Dual Ch. Szekeres' Kis Szereto, the first Vizsla bitch to hold both titles.

Paul Sabo with American and Canadian Field Ch. Ripp Barat.

Haans V. Selle and his owner, Dr. Richard Reinhardt.

The late Count Bela Hadik with Ch. Hunor.

# The Vizsla in the Field

One of the first outstanding Vizslas to run in the field was Dr. I. S. Osborn's imported "little red dog," Rex, S.G. The "Sehr Gut" rating had been awarded in European trials. Bela Hadik remembers him as "the most beautiful running dog in the late fifties. I know that he and Nikki's Arco won most of the field trials out west. . . ."*

The first field trial of the Magyar Vizsla Club of America was held on September 25, 1955, at Fort Snelling, Minnesota. The judges were Fred Schultz and Joseph Deiss. Gingo Von Schloss Loosdorf, owned by William Olson and Jack Hatfield, won the shooting dog stake after a run-off with Dr. Osborn's Broc Olca. The derby stake was taken by Rakk Selle, owned by Osborn and handled by Paul Sabo. Winner of the puppy stake was Charles Hunt's Csicskas of Goncoltanya, handled by Jeno Dus. (Csicskas died on September 21, 1971, at the age of seventeen.)

Rex Selle is the single most important foundation sire in the history of the breed in America. At the 1957 National Trial, four of the nine winners were sired by him. Rakk Selle and a top-drawer bitch, Iskra Kubis, were two more top-running dogs which Osborn imported. Another Osborn import, Broc Olca, exceeded Rex Selle's winning record. Broc Olca's great contribution to the breed is as sire of American and Canadian Field Champion Ripp Barat. Broc Olca is also the great-grandsire of the first Vizsla Best-in-Show winner, American, Canadian, and Mexican Champion Napkelte Vadasz Dalos, bred by Dr. Phil Wright of Ontario, Canada. Ripp Barat won the national club trials in 1960, 1961, and 1962. He was campaigned by Paul Sabo for his owner, Betty Kenly of Phoenix, Arizona. During his extensive field campaign, he was co-owned by Dr. and Mrs. William Meminger of Erie, Pennsylvania. Mrs. Meminger was the first A.K.C. licensed Vizsla judge-specialist (that is, the first Vizsla breeder and owner licensed to judge the breed).

Ripp Barat, mated to Rakk Selle's daughter Sissy Selle, produced one of the most famous litters of all time for his breeder, Betty Kenly. Three of the male puppies grew up to be American and Canadian field champions: Ripp Barat's Rippy, owned by Bob Hol-

*From correspondence with the authors.

23

comb and Paul Sabo; Ch. Gypsy Bronze Bomber, winner of the first Vizsla Club of America Specialty Show in 1965 and owned by Mrs. Harriet Anderson of Chicago; and Ch. Puerco Pete Barat, owned by the authors. Pete died at the early age of six years, but his eighteen champion get make him the top sire in the breed. Two litter mates of these outstanding dogs are Ch. Kensalon Molly Barat, owned by J. W. Lansdowne, and Ch. Silver Cholla Cactus, owned by Bob Holcomb.

Paul Sabo, who hunted and trained sporting dogs in the States and summered and trained in Saskatchewan for twenty-five successive years, considers Ripp Barat the greatest Vizsla in the field, bar none. "His deed and pedigree will be looked upon as the greatest dog of the breed in years to come, long after he has gone to his reward. All the four dozen or so litters of Ripp show this high intensity (high heads and tails while working) despite the fact that he has been bred in the years past to some of the most mediocre bitches. This is something I have decided to not let happen again, simply to forestall the possibility of any blemish to dull this great sire's background.

"I developed Rakk Selle, who was in my care for over four years. Between Rakk and Ripp, there is little choice. Neither knew that they were Vizlas and gave pointer and setter dogs in shooting dog stakes, as well as their owners, plenty of concern, whenever competing against them. Ripp has over seventy-two wins and placements in A.K.C., C.K.C., American Field, and European competition; over half of these are Firsts—quite a record for any breed. Rakk Selle also has almost equaled this record, but unfortunately for him, he lived and competed prior to the recognition of the breed by any organization other than the American Field.

"The other Vizsla whose performance in these same field trials endears him to me, is Ripp Barat's son, Ripp Barat's Rippy, who is still with me at seven years of age. He has amassed over forty-two wins and placements in the same competition as his sire, Ripp. However, due to my getting too old to make most of the trials he might have competed in, he has been 'short changed' by me for opportunities. Let me say here, that as fond as I am of Ripp, Rippy has woven his personality into my heart even more. I own half of him with Bob Holcomb. Rippy is 100% completely dependable dog in any circumstances when we hunt. Just this morning with him and Ripp down for three hours, working from horseback, he found me five native covies to Ripp's two, with temperatures in the eighty degree range and he, at seven, was still going 'full out' at the end of the

Lake's Copper Belle retrieving Canadian goose for his owners, Robert and Georgia Lake. Photograph by Richard Hughes.

hunt. Ripp is ten and I am seventy, so I can commiserate with the old boy, God bless him and his kind. He is going back to Arizona after the Ohio trials to Betty Kenly to edify her love for him. He has been with me most of his life, I'd say about 90% of it."*

The outstanding Vizsla breeder of field dogs of the sixties was the late Count Bela Hadik of Chester, New Hampshire. Bela bred and campaigned the first double title holder in the United States, Dual Ch. Futaki Darocz, out of Ch. Hunor (Field Dog Stud Book, Heniu of Gardenville), bred by Robert Foster of Bremerton, Washington. Futaki Darocz was handled to his field title by Chauncey Smith and to his bench title by John and Pricilla Carter. All were Bela's neighbors and fellow Vizsla breeders.

Bela's Futaki breeding is a lasting tribute to the devotion he lavished on the breed. As of this writing, we have only five dual champions in our breed, three of which are of Futaki breeding. The first is Futaki Darocz himself; the second is his son, Dual Ch. Bobo Buck Selle, out of Konya V. Selle, bred by Dr. Richard Reinhardt, and owned and campaigned by Sylvester Armstead of Omaha; and the third is his daughter, Dual Ch. Szekeres' Kis Szereto, out of Ch. Szekeres' Kezdet, bred by John and Pricilla Carter, and owned and campaigned by Chauncey and Carol Smith. It is interesting to note that these dual dogs were all amateur handled to their titles against professional competition. In addition to the dual champions noted, two more Futaki dogs have achieved their field titles: Field Ch. Futaki Juliska, a Darocz litter mate, and Field Ch. Futaki Jocko, both owned by Bob Perry of Acton, Massachusetts, and campaigned by Chauncey Smith. Juliska was the winner of the 1966 fall trial and received the Count Lazslo Easterhazy trophy. Her dam, Piri, had previously won it.

*From Paul Sabo's correspondence with the authors.

25

# Field Champions of Record

Field Ch. Alena Von Claus, owned by Vern E. Clausen of Aberdeen, South Dakota.

Field Ch. Amber Windy Autumn, owned by Phil Rosenberg of Wheaton, Illinois.

Dual Ch. Bobo Buck Selle, owned by Sylve⁓ ⁓r Armstead of Omaha, Nebraska.

Field Ch. Brok Selle, owned by Don Anderson of Dillon, Colorado (first field champion in the breed).

Dual Ch. Brook's Amber Mist, owned by Anthony J. Lucas of Westmont, Illinois.

Field Ch. Bullet V. Selle, owned by Tom Pratt of Clarion, Iowa.

Field Ch. Chip Odysseus, owned by Kathy Hartl of Durant, Iowa.

Dual Ch. Futaki Darocz, owned by the late Count Bela Hadik of Chester, New Hampshire (first dual champion in the breed).

Field Ch. Futaki Jocko, owned by Bob Perry of Acton, Massachusetts.

Field Ch. Futaki Juliska, owned by Bob Perry of Acton, Massachusetts.

Field Ch. Hubertus Aprod, owned by Denis Burjan of Neshanic Station, New Jersey.

Field Ch. Jake Jacaranda, owned by Len Hartl of Durant, Iowa.

Field Ch. Jodo Red, owned by Jim Rose of Boulder, Colorado.

Field Ch. Jodi of Czuki Barat, owned by Lew and Sharon Simon of Antioch, Illinois.

Field Ch. Osborn's Starfire, owned by Dr. I. S. Osborn of Le Sueur, Minnesota (first bitch field champion in the breed).

Field Ch. Rebel Rouser Duke, owned by Hank Rozanek of Norfolk, Nebraska.

Am. and Can. Field Ch. Ripp Barat, owned by Betty Kenly of Phoenix, Arizona.

Am. and Can. Field Ch. Ripp Barat's Rippy, owned by Bob Holcomb of Englewood, Colorado, and Paul Sabo of Waynesboro, Georgia. (First American and Canadian field champion in the breed and first Vizsla in Canada to win the field title.)

Field Ch. Sir Lancelot, owned by Bill Goodman of Orange, New Jersey.

Dual Ch. Szekeres' Kis Szereto, owned by Chauncey and Carol Smith of Chester, New Hampshire (first bitch dual champion in the breed).

Field Ch. Weedy Creek Dutchess, owned by Hank Rozanek of Norfolk, Nebraska.

Dual Ch. Weedy Creek Lobo, owned by Harold Wingerter of Muscatine, Iowa.

The first Canadian dog to achieve the field and bench titles is Canadian Dual Champion Rigo Von Klein, owned by Eugene Klein of British Columbia, Canada.

One of the judges at the November 1963 Vizsla National Field Trial, Ray Miller of Grand Island, Nebraska, summed up the Vizsla's performance in the field this way: "I am more than pleased with what I could see of the breed. . . . I had never seen them run before. The Vizsla seems to have such a fine temperament; the dogs want to please their handlers, and do it merrily. That is what the average hunter wants, a smart, easy handling dog to work with the handler and the gunner. In other words, a cooperating pair, as was demonstrated to me in quite a few braces."*

The Hungarian breeders developed a dog of great versatility. He can track game with the thoroughness of the hounds. He has a dominant natural instinct to point and retrieve birds, second to no other sporting breed. And in addition, he has the strength and fearlessness to brave rough and icy water to retrieve waterfowl. His superb nose proves ideal for man-trailing and tracking work.

In the United States the Vizsla really comes into his own on upland game. He is both pointer and retriever. He is fast, extremely birdy, and points by natural instinct. He has a very soft mouth that never mars the game bird, even when it is wounded. As a hunter, you will find that the outstanding feature of the Vizsla is his desire to hunt with you and for you. You will never lose him or find him in the next county hunting for himself. This aspect is directly connected with his personality. Because of his nature, he wants to be with you. However, this same attribute has come in for criticism at the mixed-breed field trials. Paul Sabo, in the early sixties, got the reaction from judges at these events that Ripp and Rippy were the exception and that most Vizslas were too short in their range. The same judges, however, acclaimed the breed for its superior nose and excellent heads-up, tails-up execution on point.

Performance expected of the Vizsla in the field is as follows:

*Puppy Performance (6 to 15 months of age)*

Puppies should be judged on instinct to hunt, desire to get out and search for scent, and have a good nose and manageable disposition. They should possess good style and appearance in the field and should find birds. Puppies will not be shot over at trials.

*Derby Performance (6 to 24 months of age)*

Derby dogs are expected to get out and search industriously for game and to exhibit bird sense, pace, range, stamina, independence, and a good nose. They are expected to point game accurately and

*December 1963 "Vizsla News," edited by Jane Graff.

27

First twin title holder in America, Dual Ch. Futaki Darocz, owned by the late Count Bela Hadik.

staunchly, though not necessarily to give a finished performance. In shoot-to-kill derby stakes, a retrieve is required but the dog is not expected to be steady to wing and shot. A derby dog which does exhibit the latter characteristics will be given due credit for this advanced type of performance.

*All-Age Performance (Amateur Gun Dog, Open, and Limited All-Age)*

Ground work is evaluated for intelligent search, range, and pace. Bird work is evaluated for accurate and quick location, pointing, and style. Training is evaluated for hunting to the course, responding to the handler, steadiness (where required), and retrieving (where required).

*Handling*: Dogs should hunt naturally and those that do so with the least amount of handling should get credit over dogs requiring continuous voice or whistle commands in order to maintain contact with the handler. It is the business of a broken dog to keep track of his handler.

*Range, Pace, and Search*: An experienced pheasant dog should search all areas in such a way as to cover all likely spots thoroughly and quickly, adapting his range to the nature of the area. Range is to be the exemplification of the instinctive urge or desire to find game. After the initial cast, dogs should hunt their way out. Dogs are to apply their range intelligently with due regard to cover and objectives rather than with regard only to distances from the handler—which could be out too far or in too close.

Grey Oaks Antonia, owned by Frank and Rose Housky.

*Finding Birds*: Dogs are not to be rated by the number of birds found or pointed, alone. The kind of finds and points made should be considered. Preferences should be given to the dog that goes boldly to a point on body scent rather than one that potters on foot scent. Difficult finds which result from intelligent searching are to be evaluated more highly than those that did not require much knowledge, bird sense, or diligence.

*Location of Birds*: Dogs which move with birds that are moving and which continue to get the bird's body scent are to be given credit for such work over a dog that holds fast to the original point even if the birds have moved beyond the reach of his nose. Such situations demonstrate the dog's ability to match wits with the birds. The accurate location of game is desired.

*Performance, Manners, and Bird Finding*: It is desirable that the winner not be charged with errors. It is preferred, however, to award a placement to a dog that displays the characteristics of style, pace, drive, bird sense, etc., even though such a dog is charged with some kind of minor error or breach of manners, rather than to award a placement to a dog lacking many of the desirable characteristics—even though an old plugger with a high bird score has no errors.

*Steadiness on Point*: Dogs are expected not to move on flush, shot, or falling game, but are to remain steady. Dogs on point are expected to remain steady until birds are flushed and shot is fired. They must not move again until ordered to do so by the handler. Upon a distinct pause of several seconds after game has fallen, the handler is then to command his dog to retrieve. This work is required to demonstrate the steadiness to fallen game and the ability to complete a satisfactory retrieve. Dogs that break shot are to be penalized for the offense (but not scratched). Following the completion of handling a find, it will be permissible for the handler to heel his dog before sending him on, in order to divert his attention from the birds just handled.

*Style and Point*: Intensity is the most desirable characteristic of a pointing dog and is therefore far more important than the position of the head or tail, though loftiness is desirable of a dog on point.

*Backing*: Dogs are expected to back a bracemate's point, whether on sight or command.

*Correction*: Correction of the dog by the handler is also forbidden. Failure to adhere to this rule may cost the dog a placement or disqualify him in the stake.

Ch. Glen Cottage Loki Barat, C.D., showing aggressive form.

Head study of Ch. Count Jonish Mignotte, owned by Elizabeth Mignotte of Canada.

Ch. Lucky-E's Hunt 'N Fun, C.D.X., T.D., is shown at the end of the track, having retrieved his object.

# The Vizsla in Obedience Competition

The Vizsla was entered in obedience trials in the United States long before the breed was recognized by the A.K.C. for conformation competition. The Vizsla is an ideal dog for obedience training because of his intelligence combined with his wish to please.

The achievement of Glen Cottage Dina, owned by Joe and Naomi Goldstein of Cary, North Carolina, is outstanding but not untypical of our breed. Dina competed at just three shows and got her C.D. at ten months of age. She also took her first major at her first show, where she qualified for her obedience degree. Dina achieved her championship at just over a year of age. Our own Ch. Glen Cottage Max Selle, at ten years of age, still responds effortlessly to commands learned at an eight-weeks obedience training class when he was a puppy.

The reader has probably noticed the liberal sprinkling of obedience degrees in the previous chapters. It is rewarding to find so many Vizsla owners dedicated to the principles of the Vizsla Club of America charter, where equal emphasis is placed on show, field, and obedience work.

As an affectionate and protective companion, the Vizsla stands among the first rank in dogdom. A Vizsla, Teko, was one of the five dog heroes of the year in the early sixties. Teko is owned by Mr. and Mrs. William Hostetler of Bloomington, Minnesota. One hot September afternoon, their two-year-old son, Johnny, left his yard and went wandering off to a neighbor's farm. He found a pond and waded in up to his shoulders when his feet stuck in the muddy bottom. Teko ran for help and found a man about a hundred yards away. Teko pawed his trousers, barked, and ran back and forth until the man followed and pulled Johnny to safety.

Jack Hatfield of Minnesota, a long-time advocate of the use of tracking dogs in police search work, has helped the St. Paul police locate missing persons. In 1964 one of his Vizslas found the body of a missing man in only twenty-five minutes. Because of his superior nose, the Vizsla was given the scent from an article of clothing and went right to work, tracking the trail through a densely wooded area to the body, which was hidden under a cover of boughs and concealed from the air by a thick pine tree.

During the same period, Scoutmaster Gaza Katona's troop was called out to help police, firemen, and volunteers search for an elderly man who had wandered from his home. Acting on an impulse, Gaza took his Vizsla, Frici, along. Frici was given the scent from the man's clothing at his home and then was encouraged to trail. Frici led the troop two miles down an abandoned railroad track, where his search culminated in success. The old man was found on the track, unable to move because of a broken thigh. Frici had never received any tracking training nor had he had any similar experience in performing his instinctive search.

The T.D. or Tracking Dog degree is the most prized and the most difficult degree to achieve of all the titles a dog can earn. The difficulty lies not so much in the dog's inability to perform, as in the technical requirements in training the dog and in gaining entry in a tracking trial.

To date, five Vizslas have achieved the T.D. degree. They are Elwain Minu Siresht, T.D., owned by Irene McElwain; Ch. Lucky-E's Hunt 'N Fun, C.D.X., T.D., owned by Jeannette and Darrell Everett; Gypsys Jason of Angelus, T.D., owned by Russell and Nancy Moon; Madigen's Lucky-E's Ruff 'N Ready, T.D., owned by Tom and Roberta Madigan; and Woodlands Bajoes V. Hunt, C.D., T.D., owned by Don and Hazel Penny.

Judge Herb Clark working with his Ch. Golden Rust's Kernel, C.D.X.

# Grooming and
# General Coat Care

Although coat types, textures, and patterns may seem purely arbitrary matters of little consequence, they are among the important characteristics that distinguish one breed from another. Actually, each breed has been developed to serve a specific purpose, and the coat that is considered typical for the breed is also the one most appropriate for the dog's specialized use—be it as guard, hunting companion, herder, or pet. A knowledge of the breed Standard approved by The American Kennel Club is helpful to the owner who takes pride in owning a well-groomed dog, typical of its breed.

Dogs with short, smooth coats (such as the Weimaraner, Basset, Beagle, smooth Dachshund and Chihuahua) usually shed only moderately and their coats require little routine grooming other than thorough brushing with a bristle brush or hound glove. For exhibition in the show ring, the whiskers, or "feelers," are trimmed close to the muzzle, but no other trimming is needed.

The wire coat of the Airedale, Wire Fox Terrier, Miniature Schnauzer, or Wirehaired Dachshund should be stripped or plucked in show trim at regular intervals. The dog can then be kept well groomed by thorough combing and brushing.

Curly coated breeds such as the Curly Coated Retriever, and the American and Irish Water Spaniels, generally require no special coat care other than frequent brushing. True curly coated breeds are very curly indeed and are not to be confused with breeds such as the Golden Retriever, Gordon Setter, Brittany Spaniel, and English Springer Spaniel, which have slightly curled or wavy coats of somewhat silky texture. The longer hair, or "feathers," typically found on tail, legs, ears, and chest of these breeds should be trimmed slightly to make the outline neater.

(UPPER LEFT) Wire brush (RIGHT) Bristle brush
(LOWER LEFT) Comb—Hound glove.

They are not "trimmed to pattern," however, as are such long-haired breeds as the Kerry Blue Terrier and the Poodle, which, when shown in the breed ring, must be clipped and trimmed in the patterns specified in the breed Standards.

The Longhaired Dachshund, the Borzoi, and the Yorkshire Terrier have long but comparatively silky coats, whereas the Newfoundland and the Rough Collie have long straight coats with rather harsh texture. Long coats must be kept brushed out thoroughly to eliminate mats and snarls.

The dog should be taught from puppyhood that a grooming session is a time for business, not for play. He should be handled gently, though, for it is essential to avoid hurting him in any way. Grooming time should be pleasant for both dog and master.

Tools required vary with the breed, but always include combs, brushes, and nail clippers and files. Combs should have wide-spaced teeth with rounded ends so that the dog's skin will not be scratched accidentally. For the same reason, brushes with natural bristles are usually preferable to those with synthetic bristles that may be too fine and sharp.

A light, airy, pleasant place in which to work is desirable, and it is of the utmost importance that neither dog nor master be distracted by other dogs, cats, or people. Consequently, it is usually preferable that grooming be done indoors.

Particularly for large or medium breeds, a sturdy grooming table is desirable. Many owners hold small puppies or Toy dogs during grooming sessions, athough it is better if they, too, are groomed on a table. Large and medium size dogs should be taught to jump onto the table and to jump off again when grooming is completed. Small dogs must be lifted on and off to avoid falls and possible injury. The dog should stand while the back and upper portions of the body are groomed, and lie on his side while underparts of his body are brushed, nails clipped, etc.

Before each session, the dog should be permitted to relieve himself. Once grooming is begun, it is important to avoid keeping the dog standing so long that he becomes tired. If a good deal of grooming is needed, it should be done in two or more short periods.

It is almost impossible to brush too much, and show dogs are often brushed for a full half hour a day, year round. If you cannot brush your dog every day, you should brush him a minimum of two or three times a week. Brushing removes loose skin particles and stimulates circulation, thereby improving condition of the skin. It also stimulates secretion of the natural skin oils that make the coat look healthy and beautiful.

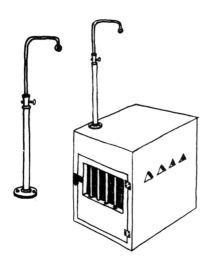

Dog crate with grooming—table top is ideal—providing rigid, well supported surface on which to groom dog, and serving as indoor kennel for puppy or grown dog. Rubber matting provides non-slip surface. Dog's collar may be attached to adjustable arm. Lightweight and readily transported yet sturdy, the crate is especially useful to owner who takes dog with him when he travels.

Before brushing, any burs adhering to the coat, as well as matted hair, should be carefully removed, using the fingers and coarse toothed comb with a gentle, teasing motion to avoid tearing the coat. The coat should first be brushed lightly in the direction in which the hair grows. Next, it should be brushed vigorously in the opposite direction, a small portion at a time, making sure the bristles penetrate the hair to the skin, until the entire coat has been brushed thoroughly and all loose soil removed. Then the coat should be brushed in the direction the hair grows, until every hair is sleekly in place.

The dog that is kept well brushed needs bathing only rarely. Once or twice a year is usually enough. Except for unusual circumstances when his coat becomes excessively soiled, no puppy under six months of age should be bathed in water. If it is necessary to bathe a puppy, extreme care must be exercised so that he will not become chilled. No dog should be bathed during cold weather and then permitted to go outside immediately. Whatever the weather, the dog should always be given a good run outdoors and permitted to relieve himself before he is bathed.

Various types of "dry baths" are available at pet supply stores. In general, they are quite satisfactory when circumstances are such that a bath in water is impractical. Dry shampoos are usually rubbed into the dog's coat thoroughly, then removed by vigorous towelling or brushing.

Before starting a water bath, the necessary equipment should be assembled. This includes a tub of appropriate size, and another tub or pail for rinse water. (A small hose with a spray nozzle—one that may be attached to the water faucet—is ideal for rinsing the dog.) A metal or plastic cup for dipping water, special dog shampoo, a small bottle of mineral or olive oil, and a supply of absorbent cotton should be placed nearby, as well as a supply of heavy towels, a wash cloth, and the dog's combs and brushes.

The amount of water required will vary according to the size of the dog, but should reach no higher than the dog's elbows. Bath water and rinse water should be slightly warmer than lukewarm, but should not be hot.

To avoid accidentally getting water in the dog's ears, place a small amount of absorbent cotton in each. With the dog standing in the tub, wet his body by using the cup to pour water over him. Take care to avoid wetting the head, and be careful to avoid getting water or shampoo in the eyes. (If you should accidentally do so, placing a few drops of mineral or olive oil in the inner corner of the eye will bring relief.) When the dog is thoroughly wet, put a small amount of shampoo on his back and work up a lather, rubbing briskly. Wash his entire body and then rinse as much of the shampoo as possible from the coat by dipping water from the tub and pouring it over the dog.

Dip the wash cloth into clean water, wring it out enough so it won't drip, then wash the dog's head, taking care to avoid the eyes. Remove the cotton from the dog's ears and sponge them gently, inside and out. Shampoo should never be used inside the ears, so if they are extremely soiled, sponge them clean with cotton saturated with mineral or olive oil. (Between baths, the ears should be cleaned frequently in the same way.)

Replace the cotton in the ears, then use the cup and container of rinse water (or hose and spray nozzle) to rinse the dog thoroughly. Quickly wrap a towel around him, remove him from the tub, and towel him as dry as possible. To avoid getting an impromptu bath yourself, you must act quickly, for once he is out of the tub, the dog will instinctively shake himself.

While the hair is still slightly damp, use a clean comb or brush to remove any tangles. If the hair is allowed to dry first, it may be completely impossible to remove them.

So far as routine grooming is concerned, the dog's eyes require little attention. Some dogs have a slight accumulation of mucus in the corner of the eyes upon waking mornings. A salt solution (1 teaspoon of table salt to one pint of warm, sterile water) can be sponged around the eyes to remove the stain. During grooming sessions it is well to inspect the eyes, since many breeds are prone to eye injury. Eye problems of a minor nature may be treated at home (see page 50), but it is imperative that any serious eye abnormality be called to the attention of the veterinarian immediately.

Feeding hard dog biscuits and hard bones helps to keep tooth surfaces clean. Slight discoloration may be readily removed by rubbing with a damp cloth dipped in salt or baking soda. The dog's head should be held firmly, the lips pulled apart gently, and the teeth rubbed lightly with the dampened cloth. Regular

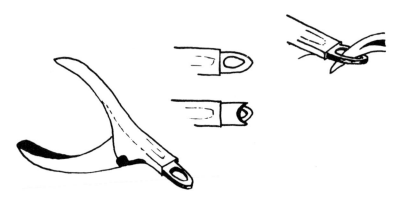

Nail trimmer—center detail shows blade cutting action. Right shows manner of inserting nail in cutter.

care usually keeps the teeth in good condition, but if tartar accumulates, it should be removed by a veterinarian.

If the dog doesn't keep his nails worn down through regular exercise on hard surfaces, they must be trimmed at intervals, for nails that are too long may cause the foot to spread and thus spoil the dog's gait. Neglected nails may even grow so long that they will grow into a circle and puncture the dog's skin. Nails can be cut easily with a nail trimmer that slides over the nail end. The cut is made just outside the faintly pink bloodline that can be seen on white nails. In pigmented nails, the bloodline is not easily seen, so the cut should be made just outside the hooklike projection on the underside of the nails. A few downward strokes with a nail file will smooth the cut surface, and, once shortened, nails can be kept short by filing at regular intervals.

Care must be taken that nails are not cut too short, since blood vessels may be accidentally severed. Should you accidentally cut a nail so short that it bleeds, apply a mild antiseptic and keep the dog quiet until bleeding stops. Usually, only a few drops of blood will be lost. But once a dog's nails have been cut painfully short, he will usually object when his feet are handled.

# Nutrition

The main food elements required by dogs are proteins, fats, and carbohydrates. Vitamins A, B complex, D, and E are essential, as are ample amounts of calcium and iron. Nine other minerals are required in small amounts but are amply provided in almost any diet, so there is no need to be concerned about them.

The most important nutrient is protein and it must be provided every day of the dog's life, for it is essential for normal daily growth and replacement of body tissues burned up in daily activity. Preferred animal protein products are beef, mutton, horse meat, and boned fish. Visceral organs—heart, liver, and tripe—are good but if used in too large quantities may cause diarrhea (bones in large amounts have the same effect). Pork, particularly fat pork, is undesirable. The "meat meal" used in some commercial foods is made from scrap meat processed at high temperatures and then dried. It is not quite so nutritious as fresh meat, but in combination with other protein products, it is an acceptable ingredient in the dog's diet.

Cooked eggs and raw egg yolk are good sources of protein, but raw egg white should never be fed since it cannot be digested by the dog and may cause diarrhea. Cottage cheese and milk (fresh, dried, and canned) are high in protein, also. Puppies thrive on milk and it can well be included in the diet of older dogs, too, if mixed with meat, vegetables, and meal. Soy-bean meal, wheat germ meal, and dried brewers yeast are vegetable products high in protein and may be used to advantage in the diet.

Vegetable and animal fats in moderate amounts should be used, especially if a main ingredient of the diet is dry or kibbled food. Fats should not be used excessively or the dog may become overweight. Generally, fats should be increased slightly in the winter and reduced somewhat during warm weather.

Carbohydrates are required for proper assimilation of fats. Dog biscuits, kibble, dog meal, and other dehydrated foods are good sources of carbohydrates, as are cereal products derived from rice, corn, wheat, and ground or rolled oats.

Vegetables supply additional proteins, vitamins, and minerals, and by providing bulk are of value in overcoming constipation. Raw or cooked carrots, celery, lettuce, beets, asparagus, tomatoes, and cooked spinach may be used. They should always be chopped or ground well and mixed with the other food. Various combinations may be used, but a good home-mixed ration for the mature dog consists of two parts of meat and one each of vegetables and dog meal (or cereal product).

Dicalcium phosphate and cod-liver oil are added to puppy diets to ensure inclusion of adequate amounts of calcium and Vitamins A and D. Indiscriminate use of dietary supplements is not only unjustified but may actually be harmful and many breeders feel that their over-use in diets of extremely small breeds may lead to excessive growth as well as to overweight at maturity.

Foods manufactured by well-known and reputable food processors are nutritionally sound and are offered in sufficient variety of flavors, textures, and consistencies that most dogs will find them tempting and satisfying. Canned foods are usually "ready to eat," while dehydrated foods in the form of kibble, meal, or biscuits may require the addition of water or milk. Dried foods containing fat sometimes become rancid, so to avoid an unpalatable change in flavor, the manufacturer may not include fat in dried food but recommend its addition at the time the water or milk is added.

Candy and other sweets are taboo, for the dog has no nutritional need for them and if he is permitted to eat them, he will usually eat less of foods he requires. Also taboo are fried foods, highly seasoned foods and extremely starchy foods, for the dog's digestive tract is not equipped to handle them.

Frozen foods should be thawed completely and warmed at least to lukewarm, while hot foods should be cooled to lukewarm. Food should be in a fairly firm state, for sloppy food is difficult for the dog to digest.

Whether meat is raw or cooked makes little difference, so long as the dog is also given the juice that seeps from the meat during cooking. Bones provide little nourishment, although gnawing bones helps make the teeth strong and helps to keep tartar from accumulating on them. Beef bones, especially large knuckle bones, are best. Fish, poultry, and chop bones should never be given to dogs since they have a tendency to splinter and may puncture the dog's digestive tract.

Clean, fresh, cool water is essential to all dogs and an adequate supply should be readily available twenty-four hours a day from the time the puppy is big enough to walk. Especially during hot weather, the drinking pan should be emptied and refilled at frequent intervals.

Puppies usually are weaned by the time they are six weeks old, so when you acquire a new puppy ten to twelve weeks old, he will already have been started on a feeding schedule. The breeder should supply exact details as to number of meals per day, types and amounts of food offered, etc. It is essential to adhere to this established routine, for drastic changes in diet may produce intestinal upsets.

Until a puppy is six months old, milk formula is an integral part of the diet. A day's supply should be made up at one time and stored in the refrigerator, and the quantity needed for each meal warmed at feeding time. The following combination is good for all breeds:

| | |
|---|---|
| 1 pint whole fresh milk | 1 tablespoon lime water |
| 1 raw egg yolk, slightly beaten | 1 tablespoon lactose |

The two latter items (as well as cod-liver oil and dicalcium phosphate to be added to solid food) are readily available at pet supply stores and drug stores.

At twelve weeks of age the amount of formula given at each feeding will vary from three to four tablespoonfuls for the Toy breeds, to perhaps two cupfuls for the large breeds. If the puppy is on the five-meal-a-day schedule when he leaves the kennel, three of the meals (first, third, and fifth each day) should consist of formula only. On a four-meal schedule, the first and fourth meals should be formula.

In either case, the second meal of the day should consist of chopped beef (preferably raw). The amount needed will vary from about three tablespoonfuls for Toy breeds up to one-half cupful for large breeds. The other meal should consist of equal parts of chopped beef and strained, cooked vegetables to which is added a little dry toast. (If you plan eventually to feed your dog canned food or dog meal, it can gradually be introduced at this

*41*

meal.) Cod-liver oil and dicalcium phosphate should be mixed with the food for this meal. The amount of each will vary from one-half teaspoonful for Toys to 1 tablespoonful for large breeds.

The amount of food offered at each meal must gradually be increased and by five months the puppy will require about twice what he needed at three months. Puppies should be fat, and it is best to let them eat as much as they want at each meal, so long as they are hungry again when it is time for the next feeding. Any food not eaten within fifteen minutes should be taken away. With a little attention to the dog's eating habits, the owner can prepare enough food and still not waste any.

When the puppy is five months old, the final feeding of the day can be eliminated and the five meals compressed into four so the puppy still receives the same quantities and types of food. At six or seven months, the four meals can be compressed into three. By the time a puppy of small or medium breed is eleven to twelve months old, feedings can be reduced to two meals a day. At the end of the first year, cod-liver oil and dicalcium phosphate can usually be discontinued.

Large breeds mature more slowly and three meals a day are usually necessary until eighteen or twenty-four months of age. Cod-liver oil and dicalcium phosphate should be continued, too, until the large dog reaches maturity.

A mature dog usually eats slightly less than he did as a growing puppy. For mature dogs, one large meal a day is usually sufficient, although some owners prefer to give two meals. As long as the dog enjoys optimum health and is neither too fat nor too thin, the number of meals a day makes little difference.

The amount of food required for mature dogs will vary. With canned dog food or home-prepared foods (that is, the combination of meat, vegetables, and meal), the approximate amount required is one-half ounce of food per pound of body weight. Thus, about eight ounces of such foods would be needed each day for a mature dog weighing sixteen pounds. If the dog is fed a dehydrated commercial food, approximately one ounce of food is needed for each pound of body weight. Approximately one pound of dry food per day would be required by a dog weighing sixteen pounds. Most manufacturers of commercial foods provide information on packages as to approximate daily needs of various breeds.

As a dog becomes older and less active, he may become too fat. Or his appetite may decrease so he becomes too thin. It is necessary to adjust the diet in either case, for the dog will live longer and enjoy better health if he is maintained in trim condition. The simplest way to decrease or increase body weight is by decreasing or increasing the amount of fat in the diet. Protein content should be maintained at a high level throughout the dog's life, although the amount of food at each meal can be decreased if the dog becomes too fat.

If the older dog becomes reluctant to eat, it may be necessary to coax him with special food he normally relishes. Warming the food will increase its aroma and usually will help to entice the dog to eat. If he still refuses, rubbing some of the food on the dog's lips and gums may stimulate interest. It may be helpful also to offer food in smaller amounts and increase the number of meals per day. Foods that are highly nutritious and easily digested are especially desirable for older dogs. Small amounts of cooked, ground liver, cottage cheese, or mashed, hard-cooked eggs should be included in the diet often.

Before a bitch is bred, her owner should make sure that she is in optimum condition—slightly on the lean side rather than fat. The bitch in whelp is given much the same diet she was fed prior to breeding, with slight increases in amounts of meat, liver, and dairy products. Beginning about six weeks after breeding, she should be fed two meals per day rather than one, and the total daily intake increased. (Some bitches in whelp require as much as 50% more food than they consume normally.) She must not be permitted to become fat, for whelping problems are more likely to occur in overweight dogs. Cod-liver oil and dicalcium phosphate should be provided until after the puppies are weaned. The amount of each will vary from one-half teaspoonful to one tablespoonful a day, depending upon her size.

The dog used only occasionally for breeding will not require a special diet, but he should be well fed and maintained in optimum condition. A dog that is at public stud and used frequently may require a slightly increased amount of food. But his basic diet will require no change so long as his general health is good and his flesh is firm and hard.

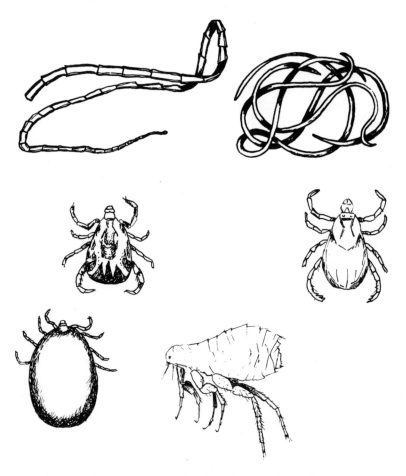

Some common internal and external parasites.

(UPPER LEFT) Tape worm. (UPPER RIGHT) Round worms. (CENTER) American dog ticks—left, female and right, male (much enlarged). (LOWER LEFT) Female tick engorged. (LOWER RIGHT) dog flea (much enlarged).

# Maintaining the Dog's Health

Proper nutrition is essential in maintaining the dog's resistance to infectious diseases, in reducing susceptibility to organic diseases, and, of course, in preventing dietary deficiency diseases. *Rickets* is probably the most common deficiency disease and afflicts puppies not provided sufficient calcium and Vitamin D. Bones fail to calcify properly, development of teeth is retarded, joints become knobby and deformed, and muscles are flabby. Symptoms include lameness, arching of neck and back, and a tendency of the legs to bow. Treatment consists of providing adequate amounts of dicalcium phosphate and Vitamin D and exposing the dog to sunlight. If detected and treated before reaching an advanced stage, bone damage may be lessened somewhat, although it cannot be corrected completely.

*Osteomalacia,* similar to rickets, may occur in adult dogs. Treatment is the same as for rickets, but here, too, prevention is preferable to cure. Permanent deformities resulting from rickets or osteomalacia will not be inherited, so once victims recover, they can be used for breeding.

To prevent the growth of disease-producing bacteria and other micro-organisms, cleanliness is essential. All equipment, especially water and food dishes, must be kept immaculately clean. Cleanliness is also essential in controlling external parasites, which thrive in unsanitary surroundings.

*Fleas, lice, mites, and ticks* can be eradicated in the dog's quarters by regular use of one of the insecticide sprays with a four to six weeks' residual effect. Bedding, blankets, and pillows should be laundered frequently and treated with an insecticide containing rotenone or DDT. Treatment for external parasites varies, depending upon the parasite involved, but a number of good dips and powders are available at pet stores.

Fleas may be eliminated by using a flea powder containing lindane. The coat must be dusted thoroughly with the powder at frequent intervals during the summer months when fleas are a problem. For eradicating lice, dips containing rotenone or DDT must be applied to the coat. A fine-toothed comb should then be used to remove dead lice and eggs, which are firmly attached to the coat. Mites live deep in the ear canal, producing irritation to the lining of the ear and causing a brownish-black, dry type discharge. Plain mineral oil or ear ointment should be swabbed on the inner surface of the ear twice a week until mites are eliminated. Ticks may carry Rocky Mountain spotted fever, so, to avoid possible infection, they should be removed from the dog only with tweezers and should be destroyed by burning (or by dropping them into insecticide). Heavy infestation can be controlled by sponging the coat daily with a solution containing a special tick dip.

Among preparations available for controlling parasites on the dog's body are some that can be given internally. Since dosage must be carefully controlled, these preparations should not be used without consulting a veterinarian.

*Internal parasites,* with the exception of the tapeworm, may be transmitted from a mother dog to the puppies. Infestation may also result from contact with infected bedding or through access to a yard where an infected dog relieves himself. The types that may infest dogs are roundworms, whipworms, tapeworms, hookworms, and heartworms. All cause similar symptoms: a generally unthrifty appearance, stary coat, dull eyes, weakness and emaciation despite a ravenous appetite, coughing, vomiting, diarrhea, and sometimes bloody stools. Not all symptoms are present in every case, of course.

Promiscuous dosing for worms is dangerous and different types of worms require different treatment. So if you suspect your dog has worms, ask your veterinarian to make a microscopic examination of the feces, and to prescribe appropriate treatment if evidence of worm infestation is found.

*Clogged anal glands* cause intense discomfort, which the dog may attempt to relieve by scooting himself along the floor on his haunches. These glands, located on either side of the anus, secrete a substance that enables the dog to expel the contents of the rectum. If they become clogged, they may give the dog an unpleasant odor and when neglected, serious infection may result. Contents of the glands can be easily expelled into a wad of

cotton, which should be held under the tail with the left hand. Then, using the right hand, pressure should be exerted with the thumb on one side of the anus, the forefinger on the other. The normal secretion is brownish in color, with an unpleasant odor. The presence of blood or pus indicates infection and should be called to the attention of a veterinarian.

*Fits,* often considered a symptom of worms, may result from a variety of causes, including vitamin deficiencies, or playing to the point of exhaustion. A veterinarian should be consulted when a fit occurs, for it may be a symptom of serious illness.

*Distemper* takes many and varied forms, so it is sometimes difficult for even experienced veterinarians to diagnose. It is the number one killer of dogs, and although it is not unknown in older dogs, its victims are usually puppies. While some dogs do recover, permanent damage to the brain or nervous system is often sustained. Symptoms may include lethargy, diarrhea, vomiting, reduced appetite, cough, nasal discharge, inflammation of the eyes, and a rise in temperature. If distemper is suspected, a veterinarian must be consulted at once, for early treatment is essential. Effective preventive measures lie in inoculation. Shots for temporary immunity should be given all puppies within a few weeks after whelping, and the permanent inoculations should be given as soon thereafter as possible.

*Hardpad* has been fairly prevalent in Great Britain for a number of years, and its incidence in the United States is increasing. Symptoms are similar to those of distemper, but as the disease progresses, the pads of the feet harden and eventually peel. Chances of recovery are not favorable unless prompt veterinary care is secured.

*Infectious hepatitis* in dogs affects the liver, as does the human form, but apparently is not transmissible to man. Symptoms are similar to those of distemper, and the disease rapidly reaches the acute stage. Since hepatitis is often fatal, prompt veterinary treatment is essential. Effective vaccines are available and should be provided all puppies. A combination distemper-hepatitis vaccine is sometimes used.

*Leptospirosis* is caused by a micro-organism often transmitted by contact with rats, or by ingestion of food contaminated by rats. The disease can be transmitted to man, so anyone caring for an afflicted dog must take steps to avoid infection. Symptoms include vomiting, loss of appetite, diarrhea, fever, depression and lethargy, redness of eyes and gums, and sometimes jaundice. Since permanent kidney damage may result, veterinary treatment should be secured immediately.

*Rabies* is a disease that is always fatal—and it is transmissible to man. It is caused by a virus that attacks the nervous system and is present in the saliva of an infected animal. When an infected animal bites another, the virus is transmitted to the new victim. It may also enter the body through cuts and scratches that come in contact with saliva containing the virus.

All warm-blooded animals are subject to rabies and it may be transmitted by foxes, skunks, squirrels, horses, and cattle as well as dogs. Anyone bitten by a dog (or other animal) should see his physician immediately, and health and law enforcement officials should be notified. Also, if your dog is bitten by another animal, consult your veterinarian immediately.

In most areas, rabies shots are required by law. Even if not required, all dogs should be given anti-rabies vaccine, for it is an effective preventive measure.

*Injuries* of a serious nature—deep cuts, broken bones, severe burns, etc.—always require veterinary care. However, the dog may need first aid before being moved to a veterinary hospital.

A dog injured in any way should be approached cautiously, for reactions of a dog in pain are unpredictable and he may bite even a beloved master. A muzzle should always be applied before any attempt is made to move the dog or treat him in any way. The muzzle can be improvised from a strip of cloth, bandage, or even heavy cord, looped firmly around the dog's jaws and tied under the lower jaw. The ends should then be extended back of the neck and tied again so the loop around the jaws will stay in place.

A stretcher for moving a heavy dog can be improvised from a rug or board—preferably two people should be available to transport it. A small dog can be carried by one person simply by grasping the loose skin at the nape of the neck with one hand and placing the other hand under the dog's hips.

*Severe bleeding* from a leg can be controlled by applying a tourniquet between the wound and the body, but the tourniquet must be loosened at ten-minute intervals. Severe bleeding from head or body can be controlled by placing a cloth or gauze pad over the wound, then applying firm pressure with the hand.

To treat minor cuts, first trim the hair from around the wound, then wash the area with warm soapy water and apply a mild antiseptic such as tincture of metaphen.

*Shock* is usually the aftermath of severe injury and requires immediate veterinary attention. The dog appears dazed, lips and tongue are pale, and breathing is shallow. The dog should be wrapped in blankets and kept warm, and if possible, kept lying down with his head lower than his body.

*Fractures* require immediate professional attention. A broken bone should be immobilized while the dog is transported to the veterinarian but no attempt should be made to splint it.

*Burns* from hot liquid or hot metals should be treated by applying a bland ointment, provided the burned area is small. Burns over large areas should be treated by a veterinarian.

*Burns from chemicals* should first be treated by flushing the coat with plain water, taking care to protect the dog's eyes and ears. A baking soda solution can then be applied to neutralize the chemical further. If the burned area is small, a bland ointment should be applied. If the burned area is large, more extensive treatment will be required, as well as veterinary care.

*Poisoning* is more often accidental than deliberate, but whichever the case, symptoms and treatment are the same. If the poisoning is not discovered immediately, the dog may be found unconscious. His mouth will be slimy, he will tremble, have difficulty breathing, and possibly go into convulsions. Veterinary treatment must be secured immediately.

If you find the dog eating something you know to be poisonous, induce vomiting immediately by repeatedly forcing the dog to swallow a mixture of equal parts of hydrogen peroxide and water. Delay of even a few minutes may result in death. When the contents of the stomach have been emptied, force the dog to swallow raw egg white, which will slow absorption of the poison. Then call the veterinarian. Provide him with information as to the type of poison, and follow his advice as to further treatment.

Some chemicals are toxic even though not swallowed, so before using a product, make sure it can be used safely around pets.

*Electric shock* usually results because an owner negligently leaves an electric cord exposed where the dog can chew on it. If possible, disconnect the cord before touching the dog. Otherwise, yank the cord from the dog's mouth so you will not receive a shock when you try to help him. If the dog is unconscious, artificial respiration and stimulants will be required, so a veterinarian should be consulted at once.

*Eye problems* of a minor nature—redness or occasional discharge—may be treated with a few drops of boric acid solution (2%) or salt solution (1 teaspoonful table salt to 1 pint sterile water). Cuts on the eyeball, bruises close to the eyes, or persistent discharge shoud be treated only by a veterinarian.

*Skin problems* usually cause persistent itching. However, *follicular mange* does not usually do so but is evidenced by moth-eaten-looking patches, especially about the head and along the back. *Sarcoptic mange* produces severe itching and is evidenced by patchy, crusty areas on body, legs, and abdomen. Any evidence suggesting either should be called to the attention of a veterinarian. Both require extensive treatment and both may be contracted by humans.

*Eczema* is characterized by extreme itching, redness of the skin and exudation of serous matter. It may result from a variety of causes, and the exact cause in a particular case may be difficult to determine. Relief may be secured by dusting the dog twice a week with a soothing powder containing a fungicide and an insecticide.

*Allergies* are not readily distinguished from other skin troubles except through laboratory tests. However, dog owners should be alert to the fact that straw, shavings, or newspapers used for bedding, various coat dressings and shampoos, or simply bathing the dog too often, may produce allergic skin reactions in some dogs. Thus, a change in dog-keeping practices often relieves them.

*Symptoms of illness* may be so obvious there is no question that the dog is ill, or so subtle that the owner isn't sure whether there is a change from normal or not. *Loss of appetite, malaise* (general lack of interest in what is going on), *and vomiting* may be ignored if they occur singly and persist only for a day. However, in combination with other evidence of illness, such symptoms may be significant and the dog should be watched closely. *Abnormal bowel movements,* especially diarrhea or bloody stools, are cause for immediate concern. *Urinary abnormalities* may indicate infections, and bloody urine is always an indication of a serious condition. When a dog that has long been housebroken suddenly becomes incontinent, a veterinarian should be consulted, for he may be able to suggest treatment or medication that will be helpful.

*Persistent coughing* is often considered a symptom of worms, but may also indicate heart trouble—especially in older dogs.

*Vomiting* is another symptom often attributed to worm infestation. Dogs suffering from indigestion sometimes eat grass, apparently to induce vomiting and relieve discomfort.

*Stary coat*—dull and lackluster—indicates generally poor health and possible worm infestation. *Dull eyes* may result from similar conditions. Certain forms of blindness may also cause the eyes to lose the sparkle of vibrant good health.

*Fever* is a positive indication of illness and consistent deviation from the normal temperature range of 100 to 102 degrees is cause for concern. To take the dog's temperature, first place the dog on his side. Coat the bulb of a rectal thermometer with petroleum jelly, raise the dog's tail, insert the thermometer to approximately

*51*

half its length, and hold it in position for two minutes. Clean the thermometer with rubbing alcohol after each use and be sure to shake it down.

A dog that is seriously ill, requiring surgical treatment, transfusions, or intravenous feeding, must be hospitalized. One requiring less complicated treatment is better cared for at home, but it is essential that the dog be kept in a quiet environment. Preferably, his bed should be in a room apart from family activity, yet close at hand, so his condition can be checked frequently. Clean bedding and adequate warmth are essential, as are a constant supply of fresh, cool water, and foods to tempt the appetite.

Special equipment is not ordinarily needed, but the following items will be useful in caring for a sick dog, as well as in giving first aid for injuries:

| | |
|---|---|
| petroleum jelly | tincture of metaphen |
| rubbing alcohol | cotton, gauze, and adhesive tape |
| mineral oil | burn ointment |
| rectal thermometer | tweezers |
| hydrogen peroxide | boric acid solution (2%) |

If special medication is prescribed, it may be administered in any one of several ways. A pill or small capsule may be concealed in a small piece of meat, which the dog will usually swallow with no problem. A large capsule may be given by holding the dog's mouth open, inserting the capsule as far as possible down the throat, then holding the mouth closed until the dog swallows. Liquid medicine should be measured into a small bottle or test tube. Then, if the corner of the dog's lip is pulled out while the head is tilted upward, the liquid can be poured between the lips and teeth, a small amount at a time. If he refuses to swallow, keeping the dog's head tilted and stroking his throat will usually induce swallowing.

Foods offered the sick dog should be particularly nutritious and easily digested. Meals should be smaller than usual and offered at more frequent intervals. If the dog is reluctant to eat, offer food he particularly likes and warm it slightly to increase aroma and thus make it more tempting.

# Housing Your Dog

Every dog should have a bed of his own, snug and warm, where he can retire undisturbed when he wishes to nap. And, especially with a small puppy, it is desirable to have the bed arranged so the dog can be securely confined at times, safe and contented. If the puppy is taught early in life to stay quietly in his box at night, or when the family is out, the habit will carry over into adulthood and will benefit both dog and master.

The dog should never be banished to a damp, cold basement, but should be quartered in an out-of-the-way corner close to the center of family activity. His bed can be an elaborate cushioned affair with electric warming pad, or simply a rectangular wooden box or heavy paper carton, cushioned with a clean cotton rug or towel. Actually, the latter is ideal for a new puppy, for it is snug, easy to clean, and expendable. A "door" can be cut on one side of the box for easy access, but it should be placed in such a way that the dog can still be confined when desirable.

The shipping crates used by professional handlers at dog shows make ideal indoor quarters. They are lightweight but strong, provide adequate air circulation, yet are snug and warm and easily cleaned. For the dog owner who takes his dog along when he travels, a dog crate is ideal, for the dog will willingly stay in his accustomed bed during long automobile trips, and the crate can be taken inside motels or hotels at night, making the dog a far more acceptable guest.

Dog crates are made of chromed metal or wood, and some have tops covered with a special rubber matting so they can be used as grooming tables. Anyone moderately handy with tools can construct a crate similar to the one illustrated on page 35.

Crates come in various sizes, to suit various breeds of dogs. For reasons of economy, the size selected for a puppy should be adequate for use when the dog is full grown. If the area seems too large when the puppy is small, a temporary cardboard partition can be installed to limit the area he occupies.

The dog owner who lives in the suburbs or in the country may want to keep a mature dog outdoors part of the time, in which case an outdoor doghouse should be provided. This type of kennel can also be constructed by the home handyman, but must be more substantial than quarters used indoors.

Outside finish of the doghouse can be of any type, but double wall construction will make for greater warmth in chilly weather. The floor should be smooth and easy to clean, so tongued and grooved boards or plywood are best. To keep the floor from contact with the damp earth, supports should be laid flat on the ground, running lengthwise of the structure. 2 x 4s serve well as supports for doghouses for small or medium breeds, but 4 x 4s should be used for large breeds.

The outdoor kennel must be big enough so that the dog can turn around inside, but small enough so that his body heat will keep it warm in chilly weather. The overall length of the kennel shoud be twice the length of the adult dog, measured from tip of nose to onset of tail. Width of the structure should be approximately three-fourths the length. And height from the floor to the point where the roof begins should be approximately one and a half the adult dog's height at the shoulders. If you build the house when the dog is still a puppy, you can determine his approximate adult size by referring to the Standard for his breed.

An "A" type roof is preferable, and an overhang of six inches all the way around will provide protection from sun and rain. If the roof is hinged to fold back, the interior of the kennel can be cleaned readily.

The entrance should be placed to one side rather than in the center, which will provide further protection against the weather. One of the commercially made door closures of rubber will keep out rain, snow, and wind, yet give the pet complete freedom to enter and leave his home.

The best location for the doghouse is where it will get enough morning sun to keep it dry, yet will not be in full sun during hot afternoons. If possible, the back of the doghouse should be placed toward the prevailing winds.

A fenced run or yard is essential to the outdoor kennel, and the fence must be sturdy enough that the dog cannot break through it, and high enough so he cannot jump or climb over it. The gate should have a latch of a type that can't be opened accidentally. The area enclosed must provide the dog with space to exercise freely, or else the dog must be exercised on the leash every day, for no dog should be confined to a tiny yard day after day without adequate exercise.

The yard must be kept clean and odor free, and the doghouse must be scrubbed and disinfected at frequent intervals. One of the insecticides made especially for use in kennels—one with a four to six weeks' residual effect—should be used regularly on floors and walls, inside and out.

Enough bedding must be provided so the dog can snuggle into it and keep warm in chilly weather. Bedding should either be of a type that is inexpensive, so it can be discarded and replaced frequently, or of a type that can be laundered readily. Dogs are often allergic to fungi found on straw, hay, or grass, and sometimes newspaper ink, but cedar shavings and old cotton rugs and blankets usually serve very well.

The Stone-age Dog

A Spotted Dog from India, "Parent of the Modern Coach dog."

# History of
## the Genus *Canis*

The history of man's association with the dog is a fascinating one, extending into the past at least seventy centuries, and involving the entire history of civilized man from the early Stone Age to the present.

The dog, technically a member of the genus *Canis*, belongs to the zoological family group *Canidae*, which also includes such animals as wolves, foxes, jackals, and coyotes. In the past it was generally agreed that the dog resulted from the crossing of various members of the family *Canidae*. Recent findings have amended this theory somewhat, and most authorities now feel the jackal probably has no direct relationship with the dog. Some believe dogs are descended from wolves and foxes, with the wolf the main progenitor. As evidence, they cite the fact that the teeth of the wolf are identical in every detail with those of the dog, whereas the teeth of the jackal are totally different.

Still other authorities insist that the dog always has existed as a separate and distinct animal. This group admits that it is possible for a dog to mate with a fox, coyote, or wolf, but points out that the resulting puppies are unable to breed with each other, although they can breed with stock of the same genus as either parent. Therefore, they insist, it was impossible for a new and distinct genus to have developed from such crossings. They then cite the fact that any dog can be mated with any other dog and the progeny bred among themselves. These researchers point out, too, heritable characteristics that are totally different in the three animals. For instance, the pupil of the dog's eye is round, that of the wolf oblique, and that of the jackal vertical. Tails, too, differ considerably, for tails of foxes, coyotes, and wolves always drop behind them, while those of dogs may be carried over the back or straight up.

Much conjecture centers on two wild dog species that still exist—the Dingo of Australia, and the Dhole in India. Similar in appearance, both are reddish in color, both have rather long, slender jaws, both have rounded ears that stand straight up, and both species hunt in packs. Evidence indicates that they had the same ancestors. Yet, today, they live in areas that are more than 4,000 miles apart.

Despite the fact that it is impossible to determine just when the dog first appeared as a distinct species, archeologists have found definite proof that the dog was the first animal domesticated by man. When man lived by tracking, trapping, and killing game, the dog added to the forces through which man discovered and captured the quarry. Man shared his primitive living quarters with the dog, and the two together devoured the prey. Thus, each helped to sustain the life of the other. The dog assisted man, too, by defending the campsite against marauders. As man gradually became civilized, the dog's usefulness was extended to guarding the other animals man domesticated, and, even before the wheel was invented, the dog served as a beast of burden. In fact, archeological findings show that aboriginal peoples of Switzerland and Ireland used the dog for such purposes long before they learned to till the soil.

Cave drawings from the palaeolithic era, which was the earliest part of the Old World Stone Age, include hunting scenes in which a rough, canine-like form is shown alongside huntsmen. One of these drawings is believed to be 50,000 years old, and gives credence to the theory that all dogs are descended from a primitive type ancestor that was neither fox nor wolf.

Archeological findings show that Europeans of the New Stone Age possessed a breed of dogs of wolf-like appearance, and a similar breed has been traced through the successive Bronze Age and Iron Age. Accurate details are not available, though, as to the external appearance of domesticated dogs prior to historic times (roughly four to five thousand years ago).

Early records in Chaldean and Egyptian tombs show that several distinct and well-established dog types had been developed by about 3700 B.C. Similar records show that the early people of the Nile Valley regarded the dog as a god, often burying it as a mummy in special cemeteries and mourning its death.

Some of the early Egyptian dogs had been given names, such as Akna, Tarn, and Abu, and slender dogs of the Greyhound type and a short-legged Terrier type are depicted in drawings found

Bas-relief of Hunters with Nets and Mastiffs. From the walls of Assurbanipal's palace at Nineveh 668-626 B.C. *British Museum.*

in Egyptian royal tombs that are at least 5,000 years old. The Afghan Hound and the Saluki are shown in drawings of only slightly later times. Another type of ancient Egyptian dog was much heavier and more powerful, with short coat and massive head. These probably hunted by scent, as did still another type of Egyptian dog that had a thick furry coat, a tail curled almost flat over the back, and erect "prick" ears.

Early Romans and Greeks mentioned their dogs often in literature, and both made distinctions between those that hunted by sight and those that hunted by scent. The Romans' canine classifications were similar to those we use now. In addition to dogs comparable to the Greek sight and scent hounds, the ancient Romans had Canes *villatici* (housedogs) and Canes *pastorales* (sheepdogs), corresponding to our present-day working dogs.

The dog is mentioned many times in the Old Testament. The first reference, in Genesis, leads some Biblical scholars to assert that man and dog have been companions from the time man was created. And later Biblical references bring an awareness of the diversity in breeds and types existing thousands of years ago.

As civilization advanced, man found new uses for dogs. Some required great size and strength. Others needed less of these characteristics but greater agility and better sight. Still others needed an accentuated sense of smell. As time went on, men kept those puppies that suited specific purposes especially well and bred them together. Through ensuing generations of selective breeding, desirable characteristics appeared with increasing frequency. Dogs used in a particular region for a special purpose gradually became more like each other, yet less like dogs of other areas used for different purposes. Thus were established the foundations for the various breeds we have today.

The American Kennel Club, the leading dog organization in the United States, divides the various breeds into six "Groups," based on similarity of purposes for which they were developed.

"Sporting Dogs" include the Pointers, Setters, Spaniels, and Retrievers that were developed by sportsmen interested in hunting game birds. Most of the Pointers and Setters are of comparatively recent origin. Their development parallels the development of sporting firearms, and most of them evolved in the British Isles. Exceptions are the Weimaraner, which was developed in Germany, and the Vizsla, or Hungarian Pointer, believed to have been developed by the Magyar hordes that swarmed over Central Europe a thousand years ago. The Irish were among the first to use Spaniels, though the name indicates that the original stock may have come from Spain. Two Sporting breeds, the American Water Spaniel, and the Chesapeake Bay Retriever, were developed entirely in the United States.

"Hounds," among which are Dachshunds, Beagles, Bassets, Harriers, and Foxhounds, are used singly, in pairs, or in packs to "course" (or run) and hunt for rabbits, foxes, and various rodents. But little larger, the Norwegian Elkhound is used in its native country to hunt big game—moose, bear, and deer.

The smaller Hound breeds hunt by scent, while the Irish Wolfhound, Borzoi, Scottish Deerhound, Saluki, and Greyhound hunt by sight. The Whippet, Saluki, and Greyhound are notably fleet of foot, and racing these breeds (particularly the Greyhound) is popular sport.

The Bloodhound is a member of the Hound Group that is known world-wide for its scenting ability. On the other hand, the Basenji is a comparatively rare Hound breed and has the distinction of being the only dog that cannot bark.

"Working Dogs" have the greatest utilitarian value of all modern dogs and contribute to man's welfare in diverse ways. The Boxer, Doberman Pinscher, Rottweiler, German Shepherd, Great Dane, and Giant Schnauzer are often trained to serve as sentries and aid police in patrolling streets. The German Shepherd is especially noted as a guide dog for the blind. The Collie, the various breeds of Sheepdogs, and the two Corgi breeds are known throughout the world for their extraordinary herding ability. And the exploits of the St. Bernard and Newfoundland are legendary, their records for saving lives unsurpassed.

The Siberian Husky and the Alaskan Malamute are noted for tremendous strength and stamina. Had it not been for these hardy Northern breeds, the great polar expeditions might never have taken place, for Admiral Byrd used these dogs to reach points inaccessible by other means. Even today, with our jet-age transportation, the Northern breeds provide a more practical means of travel in frigid areas than do modern machines.

"Terriers" derive their name from the Latin *terra,* meaning

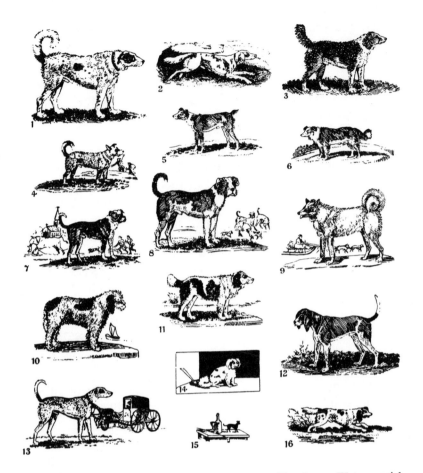

1. The Newfoundland. 2. The English Setter. 3. The Large Water-spaniel. 4. The Terrier. 5. The Cur-dog. 6. The Shepherd's Dog. 7. The Bulldog. 8. The Mastiff. 9. The Greenland Dog. 10. The Rought Water-dog. 11. The Small Water-spaniel. 12. The Old English Hound. 13. The Dalmatian or Coach-dog. 14. The Comporter (very much of a Papillon). 15. "Toy Dog, Bottle, Glass, and Pipe." *From a vignette.* 16. The Springer or Cocker. *From Thomas Bewick's "General History of Quadrupeds" (1790).*

"earth," for all of the breeds in this Group are fond of burrowing. Terriers hunt by digging into the earth to rout rodents and fur-bearing animals such as badgers, woodchucks, and otters. Some breeds are expected merely to force the animals from their dens in order that the hunter can complete the capture. Others are expected to find and destroy the prey, either on the surface or under the ground.

Terriers come in a wide variety of sizes, ranging from such large breeds as the Airedale and Kerry Blue to such small ones as the Skye, the Dandie Dinmont, the West Highland White, and the Scottish Terrier. England, Ireland, and Scotland produced most of the Terrier breeds, although the Miniature Schnauzer was developed in Germany.

"Toys," as the term indicates, are small breeds. Although they make little claim to usefulness other than as ideal housepets, Toy dogs develop as much protective instinct as do larger breeds and serve effectively in warning of the approach of strangers.

Origins of the Toys are varied. The Pekingese was developed as the royal dog of China more than two thousand years before the birth of Christ. The Chihuahua, smallest of the Toys, originated in Mexico and is believed to be a descendant of the Techichi, a dog of great religious significance to the Aztecs, while the Italian Greyhound was popular in the days of ancient Pompeii.

"Non-Sporting Dogs" include a number of popular breeds of varying ancestry. The Standard and Miniature Poodles were developed in France for the purpose of retrieving game from water. The Bulldog originated in Great Britain and was bred for the purpose of "baiting" bulls. The Chowchow apparently originated centuries ago in China, for it is pictured in a bas relief dated to the Han dynasty of about 150 B.C.

The Dalmatian served as a carriage dog in Dalmatia, protecting travelers in bandit-infested regions. The Keeshond, recognized as the national dog of Holland, is believed to have originated in the Arctic or possibly the Sub-Arctic. The Schipperke, sometimes erroneously described as a Dutch dog, originated in the Flemish provinces of Belgium. And the Lhasa Apso came from Tibet, where it is known as "Abso Seng Kye," the "Bark Lion Sentinel Dog."

During the thousands of years that man and dog have been closely associated, a strong affinity has been built up between the two. The dog has more than earned his way as a helper, and his faithful, selfless devotion to man is legendary. The ways in which the dog has proved his intelligence, his courage, and his dependability in situations of stress are amply recorded in the countless tales of canine heroism that highlight the pages of history, both past and present.

*Dogs in Woodcuts.* (*1st row*) (LEFT) "Maltese dog with shorter hair"; (RIGHT) "Spotted sporting dog trained to catch game"; (*2nd row*) (LEFT) Sporting white dog; (RIGHT) "Spanish dog with floppy ears": (*3rd row*) (LEFT) "French dog"; (RIGHT) "Mad dog of Grevinus"; (*4th row*) (LEFT) Hairy Maltese dog; (RIGHT) "English fighting dog . . . of horrid aspect." *From Aldrovandus (1637).*

# History of the Vizsla

An anonymous scribe of the Hungarian King Adelbert III (1235-1270) wrote in his history of origins and wanderings of the Magyars, that by tradition the Magyars, when not occupied by cattle breeding, hunted extensively. During this era, the Magyars had camp dogs, sheepdogs, watch dogs, driving dogs (Pulik) and "yellow" Vizslas. Among early illustrations of the Vizsla are those in the *Becsi Kepes Kronica* (*Viennese Illustrated Chronicle*), written by the Carmelite Friars in 1357 at the direction of King Lajos the Great of Hungary. Three illuminations show the progenitor of the Vizsla as we know him. The third depicts a more refined variation of the first two illustrated, showing the Vizsla as used in falconry. It is the consensus of Hungarian scholars that this last pictured bird dog was brought into the Hungarian plains by the Magyars when they came from The Steppes. No one doubts that through the centuries this basic Vizsla was crossbred with other types of dogs, including hound breeds. However, the Magyars apparently always took such crosses back to the basic Vizsla, for all hound noses are black and the Vizsla nose is flesh colored or brown, as described in the A.K.C. Standard. Even today, the Vizsla resembles the lighter wild dogs of the Russian Steppes in color and quality of coat.

Before firearms came into use, hunters used scenting dogs to search for game birds which were caught in nets or with the falcon. This is borne out by the following historical evidence: Michael Komlossy wrote on August 15, 1515, to his younger brother: "Furthermore, I ask you dear brother to send me a good retriever, a good quail dog (Vizsla)—I ask you for a good one, as my knight, Sir Janos Kotsis knows his falconry, because he has dealt with falconer Kristof Krassay and fowler Ferenc." (From Lampert, Old Letter 203 from the Hungarian National Record Office.) *

And Janos Gyulay wrote in Latin to Kristof Batthyani in 1563: "We know your lordship has some smaller hawks, too. We would be grateful for one or two falcons. But a dog (Vizsla) with a good nose, a retriever for quail, would be most appreciated." (*Sed et unum canem odoranium vulgo fyrejre valo Vizslath nobis dare velit.*) (From the archives of Count Batthanyi at Kormend, Catalogue, page 177.) *

*"The Vizsla News," Volumes 1, 2, 3 (1965).

65

International and Hungarian Ch. Csikcsicsoi Aprod with his bronze statue done by Laszlo Vastagh for the Hungarian National Agriculture Museum.

Hungarian postage stamps (from the authors' collection) depicting Magyar breeds. Vizslas are in third row from top.

Dama, whelped June 6, 1933, owned by the late Prince Louis II of Monaco. Photo courtesy H.S.H. the Prince of Monaco.

Joseph Budenz, in his *Hungarian-Ugrian Comparative Dictionary,* says, "The word Vizsla originates from a place name and very likely has Finno-Ugrian origin." There is also the old Mordvin stem in the Northern Russian word "Vesenez," to ask, search, or hunt after. Koloman Szily, in his *Language Form Dictionary,* says that "the root of the word 'Vizs' means to track, search for as in the word 'Vizslat.' " This is a sixteenth or seventeenth century word. Originally, it was used as an adjective, as in "hunting dog" or "search dog."

In the period of roughly from 1860 to 1914, when civilization had thinned the abundance of game, the Hungarian aristocracy introduced fallow deer and pheasants to the country in order to increase the amount of game for sport. At this same time, English and Moravian gamekeepers were brought in as "fashionable." The foreign keepers in turn brought in their own retrievers, which, in time, were crossed with the native "yellow" Hungarian Vizsla.

In 1880, Zoltan Hamvay, a hunter and breeder, imported English Pointers, and another hunter, Julius Barczy de Barczihaza, brought in Irish Setters. These dogs were purposely bred to purebred Vizslas and the litters sold to their friends. These two men kept the first nearly complete Vizsla studbook, according to Bill Kemenes-Kettner, a present-day Vizsla breeder in Canada. The progeny of the Hamvay-Barczy dogs are the immediate ancestors of the modern Vizsla.

In 1881, the Field Trial Union for Vizslas was established, and in 1882 the first Vizsla field trial was held on the Island of Monostor in the Danube near Budapest. The following year the very poor turnout at the trial prompted a controversy in the popular press, in which the majority of Hungarian hunters claimed that the field trial was not an adequate replica of actual inland hunting conditions. This furor caused the site to be moved to Szecheny, County Vas, in 1886, where a Vizsla bitch named Linda, owned by John Tulok, won over the male pointer, Lord of Hansa, handled by the English trainer, Barwing.

In the November 1916 issue of "Nimrod," the Hungarian hunting periodical, the Vizsla registrar, Tobor-Thuroczy, called upon Hungarian hunters to save the Vizsla from extinction. He pointed out that in the past they had been in every Hungarian manor house but because of the fashion for foreign things, the Vizsla had been crossed with too many foreign bloodlines in the third quarter of the nineteenth century. The article struck a positive note with many of the Hungarian hunters who had not found in the English and German bird dogs those qualities suited for the native hunting conditions. Too, many of the hunters remembered what their fathers had said in eulogy about the Vizsla. Additional commentaries were published in the journal, the editor of which, Ur Kerpely, was an enthusiastic Vizsla supporter. This same year, Hubertus, the Hungarian National Hunters Association, established a hunting dog division which took over the leadership in preserving the Vizsla.

In 1917, the organization inaugurated a temporary pedigree for Vizslas, and searched country-wide for those bird dogs which resembled most closely those depicted in old paintings. This monumental task was undertaken in wartime, when most of the hunters were serving on various fronts. The organization managed to register three dogs and nine bitches as Vizsla foundation stock: Ficko, dog, owned by Dr. Stephen Nemes; Honved, dog, owned by "Nimrod Magazine"; Rupp, dog, owned by Count Stephen Szechenyi (uncle of Count Bela Hadik's wife, who was born Countess Alice Szechenyi); Laura, bitch, owned by Franc Kasza; Rica, bitch, owned by Daniel Halka; Stanci, bitch, owned by Janoes Sass; Ara, bitch, owned by Adalbert Blaskovick; Donna, bitch, owned by Stephen Remenyik; Miss, bitch, owned by Dr. Ernest Kunzl; and Lidi, Kati, and Borcsa, bitches, owners unknown.

All registered Vizslas in Hungary were descended from this foundation stock. Baron Mihaly Kende, a former official of the Hungarian Vizsla Club, and frequent contributor to the Vizsla Club of America's official breed publication, the "Vizsla News," got a male puppy from a litter of Honved and Miss, bred by a battery mate in the army. Baron Kende named the dog "Tuzer," or cannoneer.

Balazs Otvos, a teacher, wrote a series of excellent articles about Hungarian bird dogs in "Nimrod" and was the first to call them "Magyar Vizsla." On May 29, 1920, Dr. Kalman Polgar, Count Laszlo Esterhazy, and Elemer Petocz, with their sporting friends, founded the Magyar Vizsla Breeders Association.

In the autumn of 1920, the association held a field trial on the estate of Count Vilmos Festetics in Toponar and drew a tremendous gallery. Following this initial trial, the association held two and three trials and one show every year. The membership gradually grew and became national in scope. In 1924, the association received a boost when Captain Karoly Baba's "Vegvari Betyar" won first place over several prize-winning English and German pointers. In 1930, the Magyar Vizsla Breeders Association merged with the National Bird Dog Club.

The *Federation Cynologique Internacionale* recognized the breed in 1935. International status was achieved just prior to World War II. Italian Queen Elena bought two Vizslas, as did Cardinal Pacelli, who continued to hunt with them even when he became Pius XII. Louis, Prince of Monaco (Rainier's father), bought "Vegari Bokrasz," who won a first prize at the International Field Trial of the Riviera in 1938, and "Potya of Hevizi," who took First in Sporting Dogs at the Paris Show in 1939 with hundreds in competition.

In 1938, Joseph Pulitzer, Jr., of St. Louis, bought Baron Mihaly Kende's "Zsoka of Sashegy," who won the Joint Manitoba Chicken Field Trial in 1940. This was the first Vizsla in America.

The Magyar Vizsla Breeders Association drew up the first Standard in 1920, revised it in 1935, and amended it in 1943. By 1944, five thousand Vizslas had been registered in Hungary. During the Soviet occupation of Eastern Europe, 80 to 90 percent of the Vizslas were destroyed. During the occupation and on through the mid-fifties uprising, the Vizsla breeders strived desperately to keep the breed going. Among the many Hungarians who left their native land during this period was Jeno Dus, the last Director of the Magyar Vizsla Club. Before he escaped, he managed to mimeograph the Vizsla studbooks and the minutes of all the club meetings. He buried the original documents and walked and crawled over the Austrian border to freedom. During the confusion of the uprising, many ownerless Vizslas were adopted by the dog lovers, but without the studbook, it was impossible to identify many of them. A condition for registration in the studbooks was that a photograph of each animal had to be inserted into the studbook, along with the pedigree.

From 1945 to 1955, the Ministry of Agriculture and, later, the Economic Office of the Transport Company of Brood Animals made registrations of dogs. New litters were registered as of unknown breeding in the new studbook.

In 1956, Kende was appointed Director of Magyar Vizsla breeding for the newly formed Magyar Dog Breeders Association. The Association registered Vizslas of unknown origin which were "very good" in appearance and showed a "very good nose." These, in turn, were bred with Vizslas having two or three generation pedigrees, and were bred once more to another dog of unknown background. All the puppies were inspected closely. If there was no hint of foreign blood in either litter, the parents were entered permanently in the breed studbook. The puppies were also registered.

Turn of the century Viennese hand-painted bronze Vizslas from the authors' collection. Photograph courtesy "Times Herald Record," Middletown, New York. Manny Fuchs, photographer.

A gap of over ten years exists between the time Pulitzer brought the first Vizsla to America and 1950 when Frank J. Tallman of Kansas City received two dogs from an American friend stationed abroad. He could not identify the dogs until he contacted Jack Baird of Poughkeepsie, New York, a noted dog authority and writer. The dogs were Vizslas. This incident and the arrival in America of a middle-aged immigrant, mark the advent of American Vizsla history. The immigrant was Jeno Dus, the last Director of the Magyar Vizsla Club, who had managed to get to upstate New York with two of his best Vizslas, Kati and Jutka, spirited out of Russian-occupied Hungary. The Goncoltanya bloodlines of Colonel Dus's Hungarian kennels were the foundation stock of the Vizslas of Charles and Joan Hunt of Tennessee, Dr. and Mrs. William C. Meminger of Pennsylvania, and the late Count Bela Hadik of New Hampshire. John Janora of West Seneca, New York, also worked very closely with Colonel Dus in breeding Vizslas during this same period.

In 1951, Jack Hatfield and Bill Olson (the latter was the owner of Waldwinkel Kennels in Minneapolis and was a former president of the German Shorthaired Pointer Club of America) were determined to bring some Vizslas to America. They had known the breed when stationed with the American occupation forces in Europe, and through secret negotiations, they were able to bring out two three-and-a-half-month-old puppies, Gelse and Gemme Von Schloss Loosdorf. They imported a total of fourteen dogs from Hungary.

In the fall of 1951, Dr. I. S. Osborn of Le Sueur, Minnesota, imported Hess Von Schloss Loosdorf and Marika Dravavology from Austria. They were direct descendents of "Betyar" and "Panni," who became the basis of Austrian registration. However, these two imports had only two generations on their official pedigree and were not eligible for registration in the United States.

70

Because of the loss of the Hungarian studbook, the only studbook in the world which contained complete pedigrees was the Czeck S.P.K.P. The stock registered in this studbook were linebred based on championship field stock. Dr. Osborn was able in the spring of 1953 to bring from Hungary the first stud dog with a five-generation pedigree based on registration in the Czeck studbook. Among the forty-odd Vizslas which he imported, this dog, Rex Selle, S.G., was the only one that was rated. These dogs were registered with the American Field Dog Stud Book in 1954. The first litter of Vizslas with complete pedigrees were whelped in Dr. Osborn's kennels in early 1954.

The Osborn and Dus-Hunt-Meminger-Janora bloodlines account for almost all of the Vizslas we have in America today. In the 1960s, it became easier to import fresh stock from Hungary, but these dogs, too, were bred back to our first imported bloodlines. Almost all Vizslas in America today are shown by their pedigrees to be related in the fourth and fifth generations.

The Magyar Vizsla Club of America was incorporated on June 25, 1953, with the following directors: Frank J. Tallman, Emmet Scanlan, Dr. B. F. Pfister, Reneau Carr, and Melvin Schlesinger of Kansas City, Missouri; William Olson and Fred Armstrong of Minneapolis, Minnesota; Elizabeth Mihalyi of Omaha, Nebraska; Homer Carr of San Mateo, California; Alexander Bodo of Passaic, New Jersey; Jack Baird, then of Hartford, Connecticut; and Jeno Dus of Hamburg, New York.

The word "Magyar" was deleted from the club name prior to The American Kennel Club recognition of the Vizsla and commencement of registration of our foundation stock in December 1960. The Club recommends that the breed name be pronounced "Vee'shla." By custom in the United States, the plural is "Vizslas," not the correct Hungarian form, "Vizslak."

Hargitai Potya, whelped July 10, 1936, owned by the late Prince Louis II of Monaco. Photograph courtesy H.S.H. the Prince of Monaco.

Ch. Paetra's Dan

Ch. Glen Cottage
Fred Barbaroosa

Ch. Glen Cottage
Alena Diva and
Ch. Glen Cottage
Chi-Chi Barat.

# Vizslas in the East

The Walter Andersons of Pittstown, New Jersey, among the first successful breeders in the East, started breeding in the late fifties. Soon after the breed was recognized, they finished Ch. Roz of Rozda and Ch. Rozelle of Rozda, both out of their Rok of Rozda and Heidi of Rozda.

The Andersons' foundation breeding was carried on by their daughter, Ginny, and her husband, Anton Tinnesz, of Lebanon, New Jersey. Their first bitch, out of the litter cited above, was Ch. Gold Star Kandi. Kandi, in turn, produced Ch. Gold Star Valdar, sired by Dr. and Mrs. Maynard Wolfe's top-winning Ch. Brok Selle Son of a Gun, the Vizsla Club of America's National Specialty winner in 1966. "Valdar," a great specimen of the breed, is handled in the show ring by Ginny and at field trials by Anton. Valdar has two Group Fourths to his credit and lacks only a few points toward his dual title. He is the sire of Ch. Miska of Mount Rose, who is out of Jutka of Mount Rose and is owned by Mrs. Jean McCabe.

Ch. Brok Selle Son of a Gun sired another exceptional dog, Ch. Great Guns Joska, owned by Mr. and Mrs. John Jacklin and out of Olca Barat's Gunnersmate, a daughter of Ripp Barat.

Burt and Peggy Abrams of New York City campaigned two fine dogs to their titles in the late sixties. Burt, a lawyer, was introduced to the breed by one of his clients, Zsa Zsa Gabor, who owns Ch. Warhorse O'Jay. The Abrams' two dogs are Ch. Warhorse Miska (by Ch. Warhorse O'Jay out of Duchess Von Rankin) and Ch. May-Ray's Jodanar (by Ch. Madonna's Joaqun out of Ch. Rozelle of Rozda).

Your authors started showing the Vizsla as soon as the breed was recognized. Competition was scarce then, but we did manage to complete the titles on the first two East Coast title holders. Ch. Ripp, owned by George and Jean Yovan of Fairfield, Connecticut, was the first title holder on the East Coast. Ripp was Best of Breed at the Westminster Show in 1962, the first time the breed was shown there, and in 1961, he took a Group Fourth at the Bronx Kennel Club Show, the first Group placement on the East Coast. Ripp was sired by Dr. Osborn's Rex Selle out of Alena Hana. He sired our first litter out of Osborn's Stylish Lady, which produced our great

73

foundation bitch, Ch. Glen Cottage Diva. Bred three times to Ch. Puerco Pete Barat (whom we got from Betty Kenly) Diva produced ten champions and is the top-producing bitch in the country. Pete, in combination with other bitches, produced nine additional champions before he died prematurely at the age of six years. Diva and a kennel mate, Ch. Glen Cottage Max Selle, were the first Vizslas to place in a Sporting Group brace at the Westminster Show. This was in 1965. Ch. Glen Cottage Max Selle is one of a trio of litter mates sired by Rex Selle, Jr., out of Diva Z. Povazia, bred by Dr. Osborn. The others are Ch. Kisasony Selle, owned by Mr. and Mrs. B. Johnson, and Ch. Golden Rex of Le Seuer, owned by N. J. Moskun.

Your authors have written the Vizsla column for "Popular Dogs" magazine since early 1962, when the former editor, Alice Wagner, invited us to do so. This is the oldest Vizsla column in publication in the United States. One of your authors, Joe Cunningham, is the fourth Vizsla judge-breeder-specialist in the country.

Ch. Glen Cottage Dark Surprise became part of the foundation stock of Barry Rathvon of Ephrata, Pennsylvania, together with his Ch. Rusty Roman. Both are grandsons of American and Canadian Field Ch. Ripp Barat. Barry's dogs have sired many successful show and field dogs in the Maryland and Pennsylvania area.

Our former neighbors, Rodger and Marion Coffman of Newburgh, New York, and now of Weston, Connecticut, established their foundation stock by buying two Diva-Pete puppies whom Marion finished: Ch. Glen Cottage Loki Barat, C.D., and Ch. Glen Cottage Talisman. Their foundation bitch is Ch. Balatoni Sassy Olca, sired by Ch. Glen Cottage Charlie (owned by Ken and Pat Winters of New York City). Sassy's first title-winning daughter is Ch. Cariad's Kalon Szerette, sired by Ch. Golden Rusts Kernel, C.D.X., and now owned by Joan Worthington of New Vernon, New Jersey. Another fine bitch produced by Loki and Sassy is Cariad's Liebestraum Barat, owned by twelve-year-old Angele Marie Wright of Cornwall, New York, and handled by her exclusively in breed and Junior Showmanship.

Herb and Sally Clark of Abington, Connecticut, have consistently produced the top-winning Vizslas on the East Coast. Their first title holders were Ch. Golden Boy Michael, Ch. Rittie, and Ch. Golden Rusts Queen, all litter mates sired by Rusty's Golden Boy out of Barsony Kralcs. Ch. Gold N Rusts Kernel, C.D.X., sired by Ch. Puerco Pete Barat out of Ch. Rittie, was the Clarks' first major winner. Kernel, in turn, sired American and Canadian Ch. Gold N Rust Daredevil, U.D., out of the Clarks' Windsweep Futaki. Daredevil has followed in his sire's footsteps by taking Best of Breed at just about all the shows in which he has been entered. A litter mate of Kernel, Ch. Glen Cottage Bar-Rit Jay Jay, owned by the Clarks, went Best of Breed at Westminster in 1969. Daredevil, braced with his sire, Kernel, took Sporting Group Brace First at that same show, for another breed first. Another Kernel litter mate is Ch. Rittie's Taschi, owned by Evelyn Laurie. A litter mate of Daredevil is Ch. Gold N Rust Go Leor, owned by James Lang. Daredevil sired Ch. Gold N Rust Baron out of Gold Rust Mirle Skir, owned by the Clarks, and he also sired three title holders in one litter out of Ch. Glen Cottage Bar-Rit Jay Jay: Ch. Magyar Arany Keralynoje (owned by Elenore Prendergast), Ch. Broc Bly of Bethwood (owned by Horace Woodlief), and Ch. Gold N. Rust Country Rogue (owned by Nandor Szayer). Herb Clark completed his provisional assignments in the summer of 1971 to become the third judge-breeder-specialist.

Doris Perez, the only Vizsla breeder in Florida, has had winning Vizslas at her Capet Creek Kennels in Hialeah since 1959. She purchased Strawbridge Antal from Major Robert Perry of England, and she was able to get Baron Mihaly Kende of Budapest to find her a bitch, Cica, which she imported. Doris finished Ch. Strawbridge Antal and his puppy, Ch. Capet Antal (out of Cica). Ch. Strawbridge Antal was by Strawbridge Fico out of Adalyn Von Hunt, the first American Vizsla imported to England by Charles and Joan Hunt of Tennessee.

Dr. William and Marge Meminger of Erie, Pennslyvania, worked very closely with Joan Hunt and Jeno Dus in the early days of the breed in this country. Mrs. Meminger, already an obedience judge, became the first Vizsla judge-breeder-specialist in the United States. The Memingers' Ch. Csic-Ked's Amas Jodie, C.D., was sired by the Hunts' Ch. Csicskas of Goncoltanya out of their Ch. Kedves Von Hunt, C.D., owned with J. R. Lynch. Two litter mates went on to take their titles: Ch. Csic-Ked's Alca, C.D. (owned by K. W. and B. J. Steen) and Ch. Csic-Ked's Ardent (owned by Dr. and Mrs. J. L. Schuster). The Memingers also owned and finished Ch. Ede De Dus and Ch. Eve De Dus, while Dr. J. D. Lasher finished his Ch. Erzsi De Dus. All were sired by Devil of Shirbob out of Boske of Goncoltanya. The breeder was Jeno Dus.

Two couples in Chester and Manchester, New Hampshire, were closely associated with the late Count Bela Hadik in establishing and proving his Futaki bloodlines. John and Pat Carter campaigned Bela's Ch. Hunor and also campaigned Dual Ch. Futaki Darocz to his bench title. John and Pat then finished their own Ch. Szekeres' Kesdet, sired by Max V. Loosdorf out of Miss Olca Kubis, their foundation bitch. Ch. Hunor and Kezdet produced Ch. Szekeres' Aranyos Heja (owned by the Carters) and Ch. Szekeres' Kelet Szel (owned by Cliff and Hilda Boggs). Ch. Caesar and Kezdet produced American and Bermudan Ch. Szekeres' Boldog Rogi, Bda. C.D., owned by Carol Flieger of Bermuda. Carol writes the "Bermuda Shorts" column each month for "Popular Dogs." Dual Ch. Darocz and Kezdet produced Ch. Szekeres' Sarga Rigo (owned by L. X. Ferry, Jr.), Ch. Szekeres' Magyal (owned by Max Holland), and Ch. Szekeres' Csillag (owned by Alexander Tolgessey). Ch. Hunor sired Ch. Mar-Ray Futaki Igric, out of Piri and owned by Ray and Mary Freer.

Chauncey and Carol Smith assisted Bela Hadik in finishing Dual Ch. Futaki Darocz to his titles, and then Chauncey handled two more Futaki dogs to their field titles: Field Ch. Futaki Jocko and Field Ch. Futaki Juliska, both owned by Bob Perry of Acton, Massachusetts. Field Ch. Futaki Juliska, mated to American and Canadian Field Ch. Ripp Barat, produced Ch. Caitlin of Highland Falls. The Smiths own Dual Ch. Szekeres' Kis Szereto (by Dual Ch. Futaki Darocz out of the Carters' Ch. Szekeres' Kesdet) the first bitch in the breed to hold the dual title. Carol Smith is the editor of the "Vizsla News."

Carlo Zezza and his wife (neighbors of the Carters and the Smiths) are the owners of Ch. Pirolin, sired by Darocz out of Wag Inn's Kedish. Pirolin has thirty-seven field wins and placements and lacks only one point for his dual title.

Dr. Bernard and Diane McGivern of Staten Island, New York, have been showing and breeding Vizslas on a select scale since the early sixties. Their first top-winning bitch, Ch. Diane's Golden Karratz, by Janos Vitex out of Lady Burdee, became their foundation bitch. "Carrie," as she is affectionately known, produced three champions in a litter sired by Ch. Count Jonish Mignotte: Ch. Karratz Amber Edition (owned by the McGiverns), Ch. Arpad Jonish Mignotte (owned by H. X. Mignotte), and Ch. Honey Karratz (owned by LeRoy Camp). Carrie also produced Ch. Magyars Tundor Karratz, sired by Ch. Wilson's Pal Joey. Dr. McGivern is the second Vizsla judge-breeder-specialist and is gradually acquiring additional sporting breeds. Dr. McGivern shares the monthly Vizsla column in "Kennel Review" magazine with Mrs. May Carpenter of Carmel,

California. Dr. McGivern has been named A.K.C. Delegate for the National Club.

Lou and Peggy Magyar have been steadily producing championship stock at their kennel in South Salem, New York. Among their winners are Ch. Aranyos Virag V. Magyar, by Ch. Wilson's Pal Joey out of Princess of Carlstadt, bred and co-owned by Ralph Wilson; Ch. Magyar's Mizzentop Dajka, of the same breeding, owned by Jack and Dianne Louv; Ch. Magyar's Mimi Zem Biro, by Ch. Paetra's Dan out of Ch. Magyar's Tundor Karratz, owned by T. Del Guidice and the Magyars; Ch. Buda's Post of Zangar, by Magyar's Paprika out of Gayla, owned by Mr. and Mrs. M. Smerling; and Ch. Starshine Tisza, by Magyar's Paprika out of Tasia Harborview, owned by Gail Tamases.

Two upstate New York breeders are E. L. Bennett of Oxford and Carl Gawenus of Norwich. Two of Bennett's early winners were Ch. Misty Hills Arpad Aaron, by Broc Olca, Jr., out of Lagine's Panni, and Ch. Misty Hills Lolli Selle Barat, by Brok Selle out of Liz Selle Barat. Carl Gawenus acquired a bitch from Bennett to establish his own breeding stock. She is Ch. J'Ann of Misty Hills, by Ch. Misty Hills Arpad Aaron out of Lagine's Panni. J'Ann, bred to Ch. Brok Selle Son of a Gun, produced Steve Wyssling's Ch. Bannik's Royal Hun. J'Ann was Best of Opposite Sex at the first National Specialty in 1965.

One of the first Regional Vizsla Clubs in the United States was the Vizsla Club of Northern New Jersey, and your authors are proud to be among its founding members. Other Regional Clubs in the East are the Vizsla Club of Central New England, the Conestoga Vizsla Club, and the Vizsla Club of Greater New York.

Ch. Gold Star's Valdar taking Group Fourth at 1966 Long Island Kennel Club Show.

Ch. Bolen's Geza Belle, owned by Mrs. Connie Johnson. Geza is a top winner and one of the top producing Vizsla bitches of all time.

## Vizlas in the Central States and Far West

Joan Hunt of Tennessee is undoubtedly the most knowledgeable Vizsla breeder in the country. Her acquaintance with the breed goes back to her diplomatic assignments in Hungary. The combined experience of Joan and her husband, Charles, goes back over forty years. Their great dog at the time of A.K.C. recognition was Ch. Csisckas of Goncoltanya, sired by Pik out of Jutka, the great bitch Jeno Dus brought with him from his Goncoltanya Kennel when he left Hungary at the end of World War II. "Csisckas" was the first Vizsla in America to receive a Group placement—third at the Heart of America Show on February 16, 1961. He followed this with another on March 26, 1961, at the Hoosier Kennel Club Show. That same day, Miclos Von Schloss Loosdorf took a Group Third at the Glendale Kennel Club Show.

Csisckas was the second champion in our breed. He and Miclos were recorded as the first title holders in "Pure-Bred Dogs, American Kennel Gazette" for June 1961.

Joan's import, Ch. Annavolgi Arany, was the third Vizsla champion and the first bitch champion, as recorded in the "Gazette" in July 1961, together with W. R. Campbell's Ch. Duchess of Shirbob. The same issue recorded Csisckas' third and Miclos' second Group placement. Joan's outstanding Ch. Annavolgi Arany lived to fifteen years of age, dying in August 1970.

Joan was the breeder of the eighth Vizsla title holder, Ch. Kedves v. Hunt, C.D., sired by Jakkelfalvi Peter out of Ch. Annavolgi Arany. This dog was owned by the Memingers and J. R. Lynch.

Another dog Joan bred, the top-winning Ch. Csopi v. Hunt, dominated the show scene in the mid-sixties. Csopi's Sporting Group placements were very impressive in that pioneering time, and he was the top-winning Vizsla in 1967. Owned by Irene Butler of Florida, Csopi was sired by Ch. Csisckas of Goncoltanya out of Gellert Csintalan.

Ch. Eneri Goncoltanya, by Csisckas out of Arany, formed the foundation stock for owner-breeder Irene Landerfield of Pennsylvania, together with her Ch. Sikitiko of Goncoltanya, by Eneri out of Tanya Mojave.

79

Among the many dogs Joan bred, the following have contributed to the breed in this country: Ch. Zlatna Devojka v. Hunt, by Jakkelfalvi Peter out of Szutyi Kislany, owned by L. R. Ludt; Ch. Csinos v. Hunt, C.D., by Csisckas out of Asta Von Schonwelde, owned by Dr. and Mrs. Paul Rothan; Ch. Stelmar Cselszi v. Hunt, by Csisckas out of Elsa v. Hunt, owned by B. G. Olsen; and Ch. Morog v. Hunt, C.D., by Csillan v. Hunt out of Miss Jo Su, owned by L. and R. Magrid.

Another outstanding winner in 1961 was George Paton's Ch. Paton's Zsomi Selle, by Rakk Selle out of Miska v. Loszaltha. He took the fourth Group placement (a Third) in the breed at Central Ohio Kennel Club on April 23, 1961, on his way to attaining his title. A litter mate, Ch. Big D. Selle, owned by J. W. Lansdowne, completed his title in 1964.

Ch. Rufus v. Theron, C.D., owned by G. E. Pynn, finished his title in early 1964 after an incredible career in the Midwest with little or no competition at most shows. Mr. Pynn faithfully showed dozens of times, and took a Group Fourth at Duluth in 1962. "Rufus" always won if any competition was entered, and Mr. Pynn's faith in him was amply rewarded for he attained his title and capped it off with two Group placements.

During this same period, D. A. and E. W. Turcke's Frontier Dusty Lou placed twice in the Group in Alaska: Fourth at Tanana Valley Kennel Club in Fairbanks on May 3, 1964, and another Fourth at Alaska Kennel Club in Anchorage on May 10, 1964.

Cliff and Hilda Boggs of Springfield, Ohio, have had success with their Vizslas in the field and on the bench. Three of their title holders are: Ch. Szekeres' Kelet Szel, by Ch. Hunor out of Ch. Szekeres' Kesdet; Ch. Behi Csinos Csiny, C.D., by Haans v. Selle out of Field Ch. Futaki Juliska; and Ch. Behi Heves Hanos, by Ch. Szkeres' Kelet Szel out of Lady Vista, C.D. One of Ch. Behi Heves Hanos' top field wins was the First placement in the Open Gun Dog Stake at the Weimaraner Club of Greater Cleveland Field Trial.

Dr. and Mrs. Paul Rothan and daughter Paula of Cincinnati have been active with the breed in obedience, show, and field for a number of years. Dr. Rothan is a past president of the Vizsla Club of America, and he is also an accredited field trial judge. The Rothans are the owners of Ch. Rothan's Betyar Geza, C.D., Rothan's Rozsda, and Ch. Csinos v. Hunt, C.D.X.

Dolli Holloway of Ohio has done well with her Ch. Holloway's

Sun Victress, by her Ch. Holloway's Red Victor out of Ch. Fenyes Leany, owned by Leon and Frances Thompson.

In the Chicago area, Mrs. Harriet Anderson's Ch. Gypsy Bronze Bomber has two notable Vizsla "firsts" to his credit: he won the first Vizsla Club of America Specialty Show, held in 1965, and on October 24th of the same year, he took the first Group First in the breed. Then he took a Group Third at the Western Reserve Show the following December. "Trigger," as he is affectionately known, was sired by American and Canadian Field Ch. Ripp Barat out of Sissy Selle. To date, two of his get have acquired their titles: Ch. Triggers Charlotte, owned by Jane Graff, and Ch. Jump-N-Jill (International B.O.B., 1969), owned by F. H. Austin. Both are out of Gypsy's Flicka and were bred by Mrs. Anderson.

Lew and Sharon Simon of Antioch, Illinois, campaigned their Field Ch. Jodi of Czuki Barat (by American and Canadian Field Ch. Ripp Barat out of Czuki of Lake Catherine). Also from Illinois is Tony Lucas, who owns Ch. Brook's Amber Mist (by Ridgeland's Copper Gypsy out of Ridgelands Olca Selle), the winner of the 1970 Vizsla Specialty. Amber Mist is also worked in the field. One of her two top wins is the First placement in the Open Limited All-Age Stake at the 1970 Vizsla Club of America fall field trial.

The Hawkeye Vizsla Club of Iowa has several members who have played major roles in the Vizsla Club of America. Carolyn Arrasmith, owner of Ch. Miss Nessi, is treasurer of the National Club at present, and Alan Hahn was Regional Governor for Iowa, National Club third vice-president, and field committee chairman. Len Hartl, owner of Field Ch. Jake Jacaranda, is past president of the Vizsla Club of America, and his wife, Cathy, owner of Field Ch. Chip Odysseus, is a former editor of the "Vizsla News." Harold Wingerter, a board member of the National Club, is the owner of Dual Ch. Weedy Creek Lobo. Tom Pratt, another past president of the National Club, is the owner of Field Ch. Bullet V. Selle.

The Reinhardts of Windsweep Farm in Scottsbluff, Nebraska, had a noted field dog in their late Haans v. Selle, by Kosa v. Selle out of Konya v. Selle. "Haans" accumulated twenty-seven A.K.C. field points but just missed winning that all important major stake. He had six Second placements in major stakes. He was shown only three times and at the second National "B" Match in 1963, he was Best in Match. Haans, an outstanding sire, produced Field Ch. Futaki Jocko, Ch. Behi's Csinos Csiny, Heidi of Windsweep, Ridgeland's

Iska Selle, Futaki Orso, Rusty Jay Caucus, Dual Ch. Bobo Buck Selle, and Field Ch. Rebel Rouser Duke. Dr. Reinhardt is a field trial judge and a past president of the Vizsla Club of America.

Another top-winning field trialer from Nebraska is Hank Rozanek of Norfolk. Hank, one of three people who have more than one dog with a field title, owns Field Ch. Rebel Rouser Duke and Field Ch. Weedy Creek Dutchess.

Bill Fisher of Beatrice, Nebraska, is the current president of the Vizsla Club of America.

G. E. and S. S. Maeckel of Texas have done very well with their breeding in an area of very little Vizsla competition. Their "Sogen's" prefix has been carried by some fine winners: Ch. Sogen's Typhoon, C.D.X., by Copper Selle out of Rio Selle; Ch. Sogen's Taffy Apple, by Mr. Sam Povazia out of Sugar Z. Selle; Ch. Sogen's Tysue, by Ch. Sogen's Typhoon, C.D.X., out of Sugar Z. Selle; Ch. Sogen's Belle Starr, by Ch. Sogen's Typhoon, C.D.X., out of Ch. Sogen's Taffy Apple; Sogen's Peanut Brittle; and Sogen's Honey Comb. "Belle Starr" won Fourth in the Group at the Houston Kennel Club Show on October 15, 1967.

Jane Graff of Seward, Nebraska, is one of the most important women in the history of the Vizsla Club of America. Jane was editor of the "Vizsla News" during the period of tremendous growth in club membership and club activities. Under her editorship (from 1962 to 1967), the "News" became truly national in character, as did the club in the same period. Jane and her husband, Maurice (Bud), were early members of the National Club and have continued to contribute time and effort to promote the breed through their support of all club activities. Although Jane and Bud belonged to the original Middle Western hard core of field people, Jane recognized the need for and campaigned continuously for the principal of the dual dog when she was editor of the "News." While most Midwesterners paid lip service to the idea of the dual dog as set down in the National Club constitution and by-laws, Jane made it her business to investigate show procedures and encouraged the field people to show their dogs to bench titles. Bud also served on the Standard Committee of the National Club.

The following dogs bred by Jane bear testimony to her belief in the dual dog: Ch. Peter Fun Galore, by Dual Ch. Weedy Creek Lobo out of Lady Fun Galore, owned by Al Sulesky; Field Ch. Jake Jacaranda, by Pepper Olca out of Sirbob's Honey Dew, owned by Len Hartl; Dual Ch. Weedy Creek Lobo, by Weedy Creek Skol out of Weedy Creek Merya, owned by Harold Wingerter; and Field Ch. Weedy Creek Dutchess, by Weedy Creek Skol out of Shirbob's Honey Dew, owned by Hank Rozanek. "Dutchess" won the Esterhazy Trophy as best bitch in the national fall field trial in 1967.

The Vizsla Club of Colorado has several breeders and sportsmen who have contributed to the national scene. Bob Anderson of Dillon, Colorado, won the first field title in the breed with his Field Ch. Brok Selle in 1964. Jim Rose of Boulder is the owner of Field Ch. Jodo Red. And Bob Holcomb of Mile High Vizslas owns American and Canadian Field Ch. Ripp Barat's Rippy. "Rippy" is the first to achieve the Canadian field championship title. Jane Holcomb is the owner of Ch. Silver Cholla Cactus, Rippy's litter mate, and Betty Kenly of Glendale, Arizona, is the breeder of these two outstanding Vizslas. The Holcombs also own Ch. Bystra Csibesz Povazia, who has two Group placements to his credit.

Dr. F. Gerbode of Washington was an early exhibitor in the West with his Don Djek Jezenski, who took a Group Fourth at the Redwood Empire Kennel Club on May 6, 1962.

Dardai Csistri has produced some remarkable winners in two breedings. Mated to Kosa V. Selle, she produced Ch. Piros of Mile High and Ch. Dardai Csistri's Cindy, owned by R. Hinds. "Piros" is owned by Mrs. Anne de Bar of Mexico and is the first Best-in-Show winner in the Western Hemisphere. He took this award both days in Mexico City, March 5 and 6, 1966.

"Csistri," bred to American and Canadian Field Ch. Ripp Barat, produced Ch. Hladky Lee of Laurel Ridge, C.D., owned by L. B. Michaels, and Ch. Ripp Barat Balaton, owned by V. A. Milano.

Regional Vizsla Clubs in the Central States include the Vizsla Club of Greater Cleveland, Miami Valley Vizsla Club, Vizsla Club of Illinois, Vizsla Club of Eastern Iowa, and Hawkeye Vizsla Club. Farther west, the Nebraska Vizsla Club and Colorado Vizsla Club represent the interests of Vizsla enthusiasts.

Paula Rothan with Ch. Rothan's Betyar Gaza, C.D., and Ch. Rothan's Rozsda Kisanya, C.D.

Ch. Besa V. Debretsin, on point, with her son, Ch. Debreceny Dezso, backing. These dogs are owned by Art and May Carpenter and Gary Carpenter.

# California and West Coast Vizslas

We have purposely held the California and West Coast Vizsla achievements until last because this area has had phenomenal success in breeding top-winning dogs.

The first part of this success story starts with a great sire, Herzog Schloss Loosdorf, whose great-granddam, Gelse V. Schloss Loosdorf, was imported by Jack Hatfield and Bill Olson of Minneapolis in 1951. "Herzog" is owned by Dr. and Mrs. John Bussing of Los Angeles. Herzog bred to Ch. Frushka Kisfaludi (out of Ch. Miclos Schloss Loosdorf and La Marde Perro Udele) produced outstanding dogs for their breeders, Alex and Marian De Lipthay. This breeding produced Ch. Anglodale's Mezei Magda, owned by Jake and Mona Castetter; Ch. De La Francesca, owned by Bill and Elsie Totton; Ch. Autumn's Golden Nocturne, C.D., owned by H. Rea and G. W. Hyde; and Ch. Count Jonish Mignotte, owned by Elizabeth Mignotte, now of Canada. Jonish Mignotte was the National Vizsla Club of America Specialty winner in 1967.

Another of Herzog's outstanding puppies, out of Roka Kisfaludi, is Ch. Anglodale's Mezei Melba, a bitch who went from the classes at a Beverly Hills show to Group Third, finishing the same day.

Another part of the success story begins with two Vizslas imported by Frank Housky: Akil Von Gromback, a dog, and Romanza Von Trutzhof, a bitch. These two were mated and produced the great Vizsla sire and winner, Ch. Sandor von Debretsin, owned by Art and May Carpenter of Carmel.

Ch. Sandor Von Debretsin, bred to Lady Ria Olca (of Osborn bloodlines and owned by Mrs. Virginia Griffin), produced Ch. Besa Von Debretsin for the Carpenters. Besa was the top-winning Vizsla in 1964, as well as an outstanding producer of champion puppies. "Sandor" also sired Ch. Boske Von Debretsin, C.D., out of Csilla Von Debretsin. Ch. Boske Von Debretsin, owned by Mrs. Robert O'Brien, was the top-winning Vizsla in 1966.

Ch. Sandor Von Debretsin, bred to Tina Von Debretsin Macias (owned by Mike and Vivian Macias), proved to be a brilliant combination. The first breeding produced Ch. Debreceny Sosija, owned by Jack and Mary Atwood; Ch. Twin Acres Casador Selle, owned by the Maciases; and Ch. Koski's Radar Von Sandor, owned

Ch. Gypsy Bronze Bomber, winning first Vizsla Club of America Specialty Show in 1965.

Ch. Piros of Mile High, taking first BIS in the Western Hemisphere.

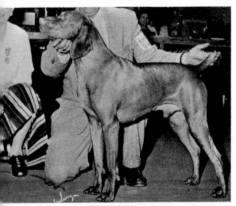

Ch. Miclos Schloss Loosdorf, first Vizsla champion in the United States.

Ch. Duchess of Shirbob, C.D., first Vizsla bitch in the United States to gain her title.

Ch. Christie Lee Woodlyn's, first Vizsla champion in Great Lakes area.

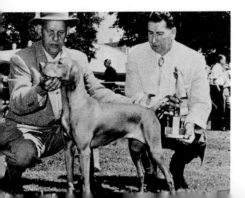

by E. C. Koski and G. B. Moore. The second breeding produced Ch. Buglair Tara of Twin Acres, owned by G. B. Moore; Ch. Jov Wasil Debretsin, owned by J. E. Atkerson; Ch. Piros Rozsa Hercege, owned by Joe and Elaine Saldivar; Ch. Debreceny Thurba, owned by Elsie Manford; and Ch. Miklos Heliker, owned by H. F. Heliker.

Tina Von Debretsin Macias, bred to Ch. Sandor Barat, produced Ch. Gaal's Vihar of Twin Acres, owned by R. and M. Gaal, and Ch. Tanja of Twin Acres, owned by the Maciases.

Betty Kenly, in addition to breeding the famous field dogs cited in an earlier chapter, contributed to West Coast breeding with her American and Canadian Field Ch. Ripp Barat, who sired Ch. Bolen's Geza Bell out of Bob and Helen Butts' bitch, Bolen's Athena. The Buttses use the "Bolen's" prefix at their kennel in Roseburg, Oregon. Betty also bred Ch. Silver Cholla Cactus, owned by Jane Holcomb and later by P. E. Zeger, Jr., and Ch. Sandor Barat, the 1968 Westminster breed winner owned by John and Marjorie Mehagian of Phoenix, Arizona.

The combination of the Carpenters' Ch. Sandor Von Debretsin and Merv and Connie Johnson's Ch. Bolen's Geza Bell was destined to produce another all-time great litter for the Reno, Nevada, couple. This litter included Ch. Batu Khan the Tartar, owned by William and Ginny Crawford; Ch. Debreceny Lila, owned by the Carpenters; and Ch. Blue Oaks Ember of Sageacre, Ch. Sageacre Piros Mihaszna, and Ch. Fleckes of Sageacre, all owned by the Johnsons.

Ch. Fleckes of Sageacre sired Ch. Tasha Z. Ravenswood Duke and Ch. Wazek Z. Ravenswood out of Ch. Tisza Z. Debreceny, owned by Ladislaus Sorokowski; and Ch. Debreceny Elemer out of Debreceny Jolie May.

Ch. Piros Rozsa Hercege produced Ch. Gaal's Kedves Voros Baron, owned by Dr. and Mrs. R. Gaal, out of Grey Oaks Antonia.

In addition to the many champions listed above, Ch. Sandor Von Debretsin sired Tom and Ann Lawson's Ch. Prince Brandiwyne out of Hassie Alena Selle, and the Crawfords' Ch. Akil von Debretsin out of Csilla Von Debretsin.

Herzog Schloss Loosdorf reenters the scene by siring an exceptional litter out of the Carpenters' Ch. Besa Von Debretsin. This litter includes Ch. Markos Von Debrecen, owned by Frank Kaparek; Ch. Tisza Z. Debreceny, owned by Ed Sorokowski; and Ch. Tartary Lulu, owned by William and Ginny Crawford. Lulu, thus far, is the only Vizsla bitch to place First in the Sporting Group. She was First in

Herzog Schloss Loosdorf, one of the early top sires in the breed.

the Group at the Dog Fancier's Association of Oregon Show and then proceeded to get another First at Umpqua Kennel Club. Lulu was also Best of Breed over sixty Vizslas in an all-Hungarian breed match in California judged by F.C.I. judge Dr. Imre Bordacs of Budapest. Lulu, mated with Ch. Batu Khan the Tartar, produced Ch. Tartary Zsoka and Ch. Huba De Sepru.

Ch. Markos Von Debrecen sired Ch. Zomar's Brute (owned by T. B. and J. L. Struthers) out of Lady Zorina of Nine Oaks, and Ch. Duke Nicholas Von Ellasar (owned by N. E. Schlader) out of Baroness Von Mihalyi.

A fourth litter mate of the Herzog-Besa breeding above is Ch. Debreceny Dezso, owned by the Carpenters' son, Gary. Dezso was the top-winning Vizsla in 1968, 1969, and 1970. He took the Vizsla Club of America's National Specialty in 1968 and 1971, and was the breed winner at Westminster in 1970.

Ch. Miclos Schloss Loosdorf, owned by Harvey Warholm, deserves a special niche in Vizsla history because he was the first of the breed to gain the championship title in America, recorded in the A.K.C. Gazette for June 1961. His sire is Gingo V. Schloss Loosdorf and his dam is Jill V. Schloss Loosdorf. Miclos also took the second Group placement (a Third) in our breed on March 26, 1961. Ch. Miclos Schloss Loosdorf, bred to La Marde Perro Udelle, produced Ch. Sergeant Loosdorf, owned by E. K. Brown. "Sergeant," bred to Ch. Barbann of Cartwright, produced Ch. Colonel Loosdorf, owned by J. Bakeman.

The fourth Vizsla champion in America was Ch. Duchess of Shirbob, C.D., owned by W. R. Campbell. Duchess of Shirbob was sired by Robert Foster's Ch. Nikki's Arco, who also sired J. A. Fife's Ch. Luko of Shirbob. Mr. Foster is a long-time former regional governor of the Vizsla Club of America from Bremerton, Washington.

"Duchess," mated to Ch. Miclos Schloss Loosdorf, produced Ch. Warhorse Cindy Bea, owned by G. W. Warholm; Ch. Warhorse O'Jay, owned by Warholm and later by Zsa Zsa Gabor; Ch. Campbell's Lady Winfield, owned by L. M. Kissick; Ch. Campbell's Lord Clem, owned by C. P. Cascio; Ch. Campbell's Brass Button, C.D., owned by D. R. Summers; and Ch. Campbell's Copper Penny, owned by the Campbells.

"Miclos," bred to Ch. Warhorse Cindy Bea, produced Ch. Warhorse Sheila, owned by G. W. Warholm, and Ch. Warhorse Sammy, owned by R. and C. Kelsey. Ch. Warhorse O'Jay, bred to Ch. Campbell's Brass Button, C.D., produced Ch. Summerarpad, owned by Dr. and Mrs. Stark.

Ch. Warhorse O'Jay, bred to Ginger Girl Von Schnaar, produced the first American and Mexican champion, Woodlyn's Tanya of Arleen, owned by Al and Irene Harris and E. C. Woods. "Tanya," bred to Betty Kenly's Ch. Puerco Pete Barat (later owned by us), produced Eva Daufenbach's Ch. Christie Lee Woodlyns. The Daufenbachs, of Emanon Kennels in Oshkosh, Wisconsin, compiled a top-winning record with this bitch in the Midwest in 1965-66.

American, Canadian, and Mexican Ch. Napkelte Vadasz Dalos, owned by William and Elsie Totton and Judy Webb, was the first Vizsla in America to take the coveted Best-in-Show award. This was at Brighton, Colorado, on May 24, 1970. Dalos repeated the win the following July by capturing the first Vizsla Best-in-Show award in Canada. Dalos, bred to Totton's Princess Tutu, produced Ch. Totton's Prince Magyar Delite.

California is the only state to have three Regional Clubs. They are the Vizsla Club of Northern California, the Vizsla Club of Southern California, and the Lone Cypress Vizsla Club.

Ch. Sandor Von Debretsin, one of the top producing sires in the breed.

Canadian Ch. Arok Parti Parazs and Canadian Ch. Egerhegyi Tincsi, son and daughter of International and Hungarian Ch. Csikcsicsoi Aprod, imported by Dr. and Mrs. William Kemenes-Kettner of Canada.

# Vizslas in Canada and the British Isles

Mr. J. Ben Jones of St. Catharines, Ontario, imported the first three Vizslas into Canada in 1955. He did not establish any breeding stock with them. In 1958, Mr. A. G. Gerle of Montreal, a field trainer, imported Vizslas from Hungary and was instrumental in having the breed recognized by the Canadian Kennel Club the same year. One of his most notable wins was taking the Open Gun Dog and Open All-Age Stakes at the Quebec Pointing Breeds trial in 1962 with his Ch. Csikcsicsoe Ari-Nora. Two of his imports became the first and second bench champions in Canada: Ch. Agres Z. Povazia in 1958 and Ch. Lyska Z. Tatler in 1959.

Dr. William and Elizabeth Kemenes-Kettner bought these dogs and with their import, Ch. Arok Parti Parazs (1962), established their Bakony Kennel in Calgary. The Kettner breeding was tremendously successful. They finished the following to their titles: Ch. Bakony Somloi Gyongi (1962); Ch. Bakony Somloi Kapitany, C.D. (1962), owned by Mr. A. H. Todd; Ch. Aprod Prucsok (1963); Ch. Bakony Zengo V. Hunt (1963); Ch. Egerhegyi Tincsi (1963); Ch. Bakony Jutka V. Hunt (1963), bred by Charles and Joan Hunt of Tennessee; and Ch. Devecseri Somloi Pushi (1964). The Kettners established their bloodlines by importing two daughters, "Parazs" and "Tincsi," and a grandson, "Prucsok," all named above, from the most famous winning Vizsla in Hungary: Eternal International and Hungarian Champion with Oak Wreath, Csikcsicsoi Aprod, owned by Dr. Paul Hetenyi of Budapest. Aprod was honored for his great wins by the Hungarian Government, which commissioned the Hungarian sculptor, Lazslo Vastagh, to portray him in bronze for the National Agricultural Museum.

An outstanding dog that was to affect future Vizsla history on the entire continent was finished in 1963. He is Ch. Janora's Pawlane Suntan, owned by Dr. P. A. Wright of Guelph. "Suntan" was bred by John Janora of West Seneca, New York. His sire was Kelly of Gardenville and his dam was Star of Gardenville. Wright's Suntan and his Ch. Bakony Csikcsicsoi Boske produced the first American and Canadian Best-in-Show winner, American, Canadian, and Mexican Ch. Napkelte Vadasz Dalos. A very fine litter mate of this winner, Ch. Napkeltei Vadasz Daraz, is owned by Dr. Wright. Another fine dog bred by Dr. Wright is American and Canadian Ch. Napkeltei Vadasz Hiros, owned by Nick and Jean Reagan of Ottawa. Another outstanding dog that finished in 1962 was Ch. Rigo Von Klein, owned by R. E. Klein of British Columbia. "Rigo" went on to become the first Canadian dual champion in the breed.

The Vizsla Club of Canada has been singularly honored for its accomplishments by the Hungarian National Kennel Club. It is believed that this is the first time a national kennel club has ever honored a breed club in a foreign country. The Canadian Club was presented with a perpetual trophy to be awarded annually to the top Canadian Vizsla. The trophy is a bronze statue of an ancient Hungarian warrior by the sculptor J. Kerenyi. The first winner of the trophy was Ch. Devecseri Somloi Pushi, owned by Elizabeth Kemenes-Kettner.

The first Vizslas were imported into the British Isles from Hungary in 1954. The first two Vizslas to make their appearance at Crufts in February 1956 were litter mates, Strawbridge Fikko and Miljenka of Tallman, bred by D. Wyndam Harris.

Evan Young, Regional Governor of the Vizsla Club in Scotland, tells us that in addition to the initial imports, another dog and bitch were imported from Hungary and a bitch, Adalyn Von Hunt, was imported from Charles and Joan Hunt of America.

Vizslas are presently shown in the "Any Variety Class," which is similar to the Miscellaneous Class at our shows. The Hungarian Vizsla Club (Britain) held its first meeting in May of 1968 and in that same year, Mrs. Kathleen J. Auchterlonie of Perthshire, Scotland, with other breed fanciers, imported Szeppataki Scaba from Hungary to improve their breeding stock.

Mrs. C. Bede Maxwell, an international judge, tells us that she was impressed with Wolfox Topaz, a Vizsla bitch owned by Mrs. Capel Edwards, when she judged her in the "Varieties" class in 1968. The breed is steadily increasing in numbers in the Isles and is gradually becoming established as a hunting dog.

# Best-in-Show Winners

Mexico City, March 5 and 6, 1966: Mexican and American Ch. Piros of Mile High; owned by Anne De Bar of Mexico City; sired by Kosa V. Selle out of Dardai Csitri; breeder, unknown.

Brighton, Colorado, May 24, 1970, and Kamloops, British Columbia, Canada, July 1970: American, Canadian, and Mexican Ch. Napkelte Vadasz Dalos; owned by William and Elsie Totton and Judy Webb; sired by Canadian Ch. Janora's Pawlane Suntan out of Bakony Csikcsicsoi Boske; breeder, Dr. P. A. Wright.

Ventura, California, July 25, 1970: Ch. Debreceny Dezso; owned by Gary Carpenter; sired by Herzog Schloss Loosdorf out of Ch. Besa Von Debretsin; breeders, Art and May Carpenter.

## Vizsla Club of America National Specialty Winners

1965—Ch. Gypsy Bronze Bomber; owned by Harriet Anderson; sired by American and Canadian Field Ch. Ripp Barat out of Sissy Selle; breeder, Betty Kenly.

1966—Ch. Brok Selle Son of a Gun; owned by Dr. and Mrs. Maynard Wolfe; sired by Brok Olca out of Bodjka Hanna; breeder, Dr. I. S. Osborn.

1967—American and Canadian Ch. Count Jonish Mignotte; owned by Elizabeth Mignotte; sired by Herzog Schloss Loosdorf out of Ch. Fruska Kisfaludi; breeder, Alex and Marion De Lipthay.

1968—Ch. Debreceny Dezso; owned by Gary Carpenter; sired by Herzog Schloss Loosdorf out of Ch. Besa Von Debretsin; breeders, Art and May Carpenter.

1969—Timarkas Tsindee of Amber owned by Peter O. Wonser; sired by Field Ch. Jodi of Czuki Barat out of Ch. Brook's Amber Mist; breeder, Tony Lucas.

1970—Ch. Brook's Amber Mist; owned by Anthony J. Lucas; sired by Ridgeland's Copper Gypsy out of Ridgeland's Olca Selle; breeder, J. J. Cuthbertson.

1971—Ch. Debreceny Dezso.

Ch. Sandor Barat                                    Ch. Glen Cottage D'Hadur

Ch. Csopi V. Hunt, C.D., owned by Irene Butler.

Cariad's Liebestraum Barat, owned by Angele Wright.

## Westminster Kennel Club Best-of-Breed Winners

1962—Ch. Ripp; owned by George and Jean Yovan; sired by Rex Selle out of Alena Hana; breeder, Dr. I. S. Osborn.

1963—Ch. Wilson's Pal Joey; owned by Ralph Wilson; sired by Wag Inn's Bela out of Bessie Mack; breeder, Michael J. Mackinnon.

1964—Ch. Wilson's Pal Joey.

1965—Ch. Wilson's Pal Joey.

1966—Ch. Gypsy Bronze Bomber; owned by Harriet Anderson; sired by American and Canadian Field Ch. Ripp Barat out of Sissy Selle; breeder, Betty Kenly.

1967—Ch. Golden Rusts Kernel; owned by Herb and Sally Clark; sired by Ch. Puerco Pete Barat out of Ch. Rittie; breeders, owners.

1968—Ch. Sandor Barat; owned by John and Marjorie Mehagian; sired by Ch. Puerco Pete Barat out of Sissy Selle; breeder, Betty Kenly.

1969—Ch. Glen Cottage Bar-Rit Jay Jay; owned by Herb and Sally Clark; sired by Ch. Puerco Pete Barat out of Ch. Rittie; breeders, owners.

1970—Ch. Debreceny Dezso; owned by Gary Carpenter; sired by Herzog Schloss Loosdorf out of Ch. Besa Von Debretsin; breeders, Art and May Carpenter.

1971—Mizzen Top's Best Link; owned by Anne and Deborah Barry; sired by Ch. Debreceny Dezso out of Ch. Mizzentop Dajka; breeders, Jack and Dianne Louv.

Ch. Warhorse O-Jay, owned by Zsa Zsa Gabor.

Ch. Madonna's Joaqun, owned by John X. Strauz.

# International Kennel Club Best-of-Breed Winners

1962—Vikingsholm Ingaar; owned by Dr. Ted Kjellstrom; sired by Ali V. Schonweide out of Asta Z. Povazia; breeder, Charles Hunt.

1963—Ch. Wilson's Pal Joey; owned by Ralph Wilson; sired by Wag Inn's Bela out of Bessie Mack; breeder, Michael J. Mackinnon.

1964—Ch. Wilson's Pal Joey.

1965—Ch. Wilson's Pal Joey.

1966—Ch. Rocking Dn's Gold Piece; owned by D. E. and N. R. Meyer; sired by Jeff V. Sumeg out of Bertha Gina Schonweide; breeder, H. R. Miller.

1967—Ch. Golden Rusts Kernel; owned by Herb and Sally Clark; sired by Ch. Puerco Pete Barat out of Ch. Rittie; breeders, owners.

1968—Ch. Csopi V. Hunt; owned by Irene Butler; sired by Ch. Csiskas of Goncoltanya out of Gellert Csintalon; breeder, Joan Hunt.

1969—Jump N Jill; owned by F. H. Austin; sired by Ch. Gypsy Bronze Bomber out of Gypsy's Flica; breeder, Harriet Anderson.

1970—Ch. Timarakas Tsindee of Amber; owned by Peter O. Wonser; sired by Field Ch. Jodi of Czuki Barat out of Ch. Brook's Amber Mist; breeder, Tony Lucas.

1971—Ch. Thora's Hau Talleria; owned by W. R. Seeley; sired by Ch. Old Weird Harold out of Ch. Thora's Hau Tascha; breeder, owner.

Ch. Ripp, first Vizsla title holder on the East Coast.

American and Bermudan Ch. Szekere's Boldog Rogi.

Rakk Selle, famous field dog of the fifties.

Ch. Csisckas of Goncoltanya, second Vizsla champion in the United States.

Dual Ch. Bobo Buck Selle, owned by Sylvester Armstead.

# Manners for the Family Dog

Although each dog has personality quirks and idiosyncrasies that set him apart as an individual, dogs in general have two characteristics that can be utilized to advantage in training. The first is the dog's strong desire to please, which has been built up through centuries of association with man. The second lies in the innate quality of the dog's mentality. It has been proved conclusively that while dogs have reasoning power, their learning ability is based on a direct association of cause and effect, so that they willingly repeat acts that bring pleasant results and discontinue acts that bring unpleasant results. Hence, to take fullest advantage of a dog's abilities, the trainer must make sure the dog understands a command, and then reward him when he obeys and correct him when he does wrong.

Commands should be as short as possible and should be repeated in the same way, day after day. Saying "Heel," one day, and "Come here and heel," the next will confuse the dog. *Heel, sit, stand, stay, down,* and *come* are standard terminology, and are preferable for a dog that may later be given advanced training.

Tone of voice is important, too. For instance, a coaxing tone helps cajole a young puppy into trying something new. Once an exercise is mastered, commands given in a firm, matter-of-fact voice give the dog confidence in his own ability. Praise, expressed in an exuberant tone will tell the dog quite clearly that he has earned his master's approval. On the other hand, a firm "No" indicates with equal clarity that he has done wrong.

Rewards for good performance may consist simply of praising lavishly and petting the dog, although many professional trainers use bits of food as rewards. Tidbits are effective only if the dog is hungry, of course. And if you smoke, you must be sure to wash your hands before each training session, for the odor of nicotine is repulsive to dogs. On the hands of a heavy smoker, the odor of nicotine may be so strong that the dog is unable to smell the tidbit.

Correction for wrong-doing should be limited to repeating "No," in a scolding tone of voice or to confining the dog to his bed. Spanking or striking the dog is taboo—particularly using sticks, which might cause injury, but the hand should never be used either. For field training as well as some obedience work, the hand is used to signal the dog. Dogs that have been punished by slapping have a tendency to cringe whenever they see a hand raised and consequently do not respond promptly when the owner's intent is not to punish but to signal.

Some trainers recommend correcting the dog by whacking him with a rolled-up newspaper. The idea is that the newspaper will not injure the dog but that the resulting noise will condition the dog to avoid repeating the act that seemingly caused the noise. Many authorities object to this type of correction, for it may result in the dog's becoming "noise-shy"—a decided disadvantage with show dogs which must maintain poise in adverse, often noisy, situations. "Noise-shyness" is also an unfortunate reaction in field dogs, since it may lead to gun-shyness.

To be effective, correction must be administered immediately, so that in the dog's mind there is a direct connection between his act and the correction. You can make voice corrections under almost any circumstances, but you must never call the dog to you and then correct him, or he will associate the correction with the fact that he has come and will become reluctant to respond. If the dog is at a distance and doing something he shouldn't, go to him and scold him while he is still involved in wrong-doing. If this is impossible, ignore the offense until he repeats it and you can correct him properly.

Especially while a dog is young, he should be watched closely and stopped before he gets into mischief. All dogs need to do a certain amount of chewing, so to prevent your puppy's chewing something you value, provide him with his own rubber balls and toys. Never allow him to chew cast-off slippers and then expect him to differentiate between cast-off items and those you value. Nylon stockings, wooden articles, and various other items may cause intestinal obstructions if the dog chews and swallows them, and death may result. So it is essential that the dog be permitted to chew only on bones or rubber toys.

Serious training for obedience should not be started until a dog is a year old. But basic training in house manners should begin the day the puppy enters his new home. A puppy should never be given the run of the house but should be confined to a box or small pen except for play periods when you can devote full attention to him. The first thing to teach the dog is his name, so that whenever he hears it, he will immediately come to attention. Whenever you are near his box, talk to him, using his name repeatedly. During play periods, talk to him, pet him, and handle him, for he must be conditioned so he will not object to being handled by a veterinarian, show judge, or family friend. As the dog investigates his surroundings, watch him carefully and if he tries something he shouldn't, reprimand him with a scolding "No!" If he repeats the offense, scold him and confine him to his box, then praise him. Discipline must be prompt, consistent, and always followed with praise. Never tease the dog, and never allow others to do so. Kindness and understanding are essential to a pleasant, mutually rewarding relationship.

When the puppy is two to three months old, secure a flat, narrow leather collar and have him start wearing it (never use a harness, which will encourage tugging and pulling). After a week or so, attach a light leather lead to the collar during play sessions and let the puppy walk around, dragging the lead behind him. Then start holding the end of the lead and coaxing the puppy to come to you. He will then be fully accustomed to collar and lead when you start taking him outside while he is being housebroken.

Housebreaking can be accomplished in a matter of approximately two weeks provided you wait until the dog is mature enough to have some control over bodily functions. This is usually at about four months. Until that time, the puppy should spend most of his day confined to his penned area, with the floor covered with several thicknesses of newspapers so that he may relieve himself when necessary without damage to floors.

Either of two methods works well in housebreaking—the choice depending upon where you live. If you live in a house with a readily accessible yard, you will probably want to train the puppy from the beginning to go outdoors. If you live in an apartment without easy access to a yard, you may decide to train him first to relieve himself on newspapers and then when he has learned control, to teach the puppy to go outdoors.

If you decide to train the puppy by taking him outdoors, arrange some means of confining him indoors where you can watch him closely—in a small penned area, or tied to a short lead (five or six feet). Dogs are naturally clean animals, reluctant to soil their quarters, and confining the puppy to a limited area will encourage him to avoid making a mess.

A young puppy must be taken out often, so watch your puppy closely and if he indicates he is about to relieve himself, take him out at once. If he has an accident, scold him and take him out so he will associate the act of going outside with the need to relieve himself. Always take the puppy out within an hour after meals—preferably to the same place each time—and make sure he relieves himself before you return him to the house. Restrict his water for two hours before bedtime and take him out just before you retire for the night. Then, as soon as you wake in the morning, take him out again.

For paper training, set aside a particular room and cover a large area of the floor with several thicknesses of newspapers. Confine the dog on a short leash and each time he relieves himself, remove the soiled papers and replace them with clean ones.

As his control increases, gradually decrease the paper area, leaving part of the floor bare. If he uses the bare floor, scold him mildly and put him on the papers, letting him know that there is where he is to relieve himself. As he comes to understand the idea, increase the bare area until papers cover only space equal to approximately two full newspaper sheets. Keep him using the papers, but begin taking him on a leash to the street at the times of day that he habitually relieves himself. Watch him closely when he is indoors and at the first sign that he needs to go, take him outdoors. Restrict his water for two hours before bedtime, but if necessary, permit him to use the papers before you retire for the night.

Using either method, the puppy will be housebroken in an amazingly short time. Once he has learned control he will need to relieve himself only four or five times a day.

Informal obedience training, started at the age of about six to eight months, will provide a good background for any advanced training you may decide to give your dog later. The collar most

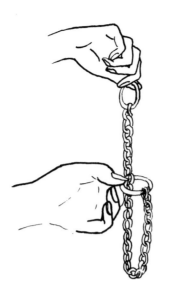

effective for training is the metal chain-link variety. The correct
size for your dog will be about one inch longer than the measure-
ment around the largest part of his head. The chain must be
slipped through one of the rings so the collar forms a loop. The
collar should be put on with the loose ring at the right of the
dog's neck, the chain attached to it coming over the neck and
through the holding ring, rather than under the neck. Since the
dog is to be at your left during most of the training, this makes
the collar most effective.

The leash should be attached to the loose ring, and should be
either webbing or leather, six feet long and a half inch to a full
inch wide. When you want your dog's attention, or wish to correct him, give a light, quick pull on the leash, which will momen-
tarily tighten the collar about the neck. Release the pressure in-
stantly, and the correction will have been made. If the puppy is
already accustomed to a leather collar, he will adjust easily to the
training collar. But before you start training sessions, practice
walking with the dog until he responds readily when you increase
tension on the leash.

Set aside a period of fifteen minutes, once or twice a day, for
regular training sessions, and train in a place where there will
be no distractions. Teach only one exercise at a time, making

sure the dog has mastered it before going on to another. It will probably take at least a week for the dog to master each exercise. As training progresses, start each session by reviewing exercises the dog has already learned, then go on to the new exercise for a period of concerted practice. When discipline is required, make the correction immediately, and always praise the dog after corrections as well as when he obeys promptly. During each session stick strictly to business. Afterwards, take time to play with the dog.

The first exercise to teach is heeling. Have the dog at your left and hold the leash as shown in the illustration on the preceding page. Start walking, and just as you put your foot forward for the first step, say your dog's name to get his attention, followed by the command, "Heel!" Simultaneously, pull on the leash lightly. As you walk, try to keep the dog at your left side, with his head alongside your left leg. Pull on the leash as necessary to urge him forward or back, to right or left, but keep him in position. Each time you pull on the leash, say "Heel!" and praise the dog lavishly. When the dog heels properly in a straight line, start making circles, turning corners, etc.

Once the dog has learned to heel well, start teaching the "sit." Each time you stop while heeling, command "Sit!" The dog will be at your left, so use your left hand to press on his rear and guide him to a sitting position, while you use the leash in your right hand to keep his head up. Hold him in position for a few moments while you praise him, then give the command to heel. Walk a few steps, stop, and repeat the procedure. Before long he will automatically sit whenever you stop. You can then teach the dog to "sit" from any position.

When the dog will sit on command without correction, he is ready to learn to stay until you release him. Simply sit him, command "Stay!" and hold him in position for perhaps half a minute, repeating "Stay," if he attempts to stand. You can release him by saying "O.K." Gradually increase the time until he will stay on command for three or four minutes.

The "stand-stay" should also be taught when the dog is on leash. While you are heeling, stop and give the command "Stand!" Keep the dog from sitting by quickly placing your left arm under him, immediately in front of his right hind leg. If he continues to try to sit, don't scold him but start up again with the heel command, walk a few steps, and stop again, repeating the stand command and preventing the dog from sitting. Once the dog has mastered the stand, teach him to stay by holding him in position and repeating the word "Stay!"

The "down stay" will prove beneficial in many situations, but especially if you wish to take your dog in the car without confining him to a crate. To teach the "down," have the dog sitting at your side with collar and leash on. If he is a large dog, step forward with the leash in your hand and turn so you face him. Let the leash touch the floor, then step over it with your right foot so it is under the instep of your shoe. Grasping the leash low down with both hands, slowly pull up, saying, "Down!" Hold the leash taut until the dog goes down. Once he responds well, teach the dog to stay in the down position (the down-stay), using the same method as for the sit- and stand-stays.

To teach small dogs the "down," another method may be used. Have the dog sit at your side, then kneel beside him. Reach across his back with your left arm, and take hold of his left front leg close to the body. At the same time, with your right hand take hold of his right front leg close to his body. As you command "Down!" gently lift the legs and place the dog in the down position. Release your hold on his legs and slide your left hand onto his back, repeating, "Down, stay," while keeping him in position.

The "come" is taught when the dog is on leash and heeling. Simply walk along, then suddenly take a step backward, saying "Come!" Pull the leash as you give the command and the dog will turn and follow you. Continue walking backward, repeatedly saying "Come," and tightening the leash if necessary.

Once the dog has mastered the exercises while on leash, try taking the leash off and going through the same routine, beginning with the heeling exercise. If the dog doesn't respond promptly, he needs review with the leash on. But patience and persistence will be rewarded, for you will have a dog you can trust to respond promptly under all conditions.

Even after they are well trained, dogs sometimes develop bad habits that are hard to break. Jumping on people is a common habit, and all members of the family must assist if it is to be broken. If the dog is a large or medium breed, take a step forward and raise your knee just as he starts to jump on you. As your knee strikes the dog's chest, command "Down!" in a scolding voice. When a small dog jumps on you, take both front paws in your hands, and, while talking in a pleasant tone of voice, step on the dog's back feet just hard enough to hurt them slightly. With either method the dog is taken by surprise and doesn't associate the discomfort with the person causing it.

Occasionally a dog may be too chummy with guests who don't care for dogs. If the dog has had obedience training, simply command "Come!" When he responds, have him sit beside you.

Excessive barking is likely to bring complaints from neighbors, and persistent efforts may be needed to subdue a dog that barks without provocation. To correct the habit, you must be close to the dog when he starts barking. Encircle his muzzle with both hands, hold his mouth shut, and command "Quiet!" in a firm voice. He should soon learn to respond so you can control him simply by giving the command.

Sniffing other dogs is an annoying habit. If the dog is off leash and sniffs other dogs, ignoring your commands to come, he needs to review the lessons on basic behavior. When the dog is on leash, scold him, then pull on the leash, command "Heel," and walk away from the other dog.

A well-trained dog will be no problem if you decide to take him with you when you travel. No matter how well he responds, however, he should never be permitted off leash when you walk him in a strange area. Distractions will be more tempting, and there will be more chance of his being attacked by other dogs. So whenever the dog travels with you, take his collar and leash along— and use them.

## Bench Shows

Centuries ago, it was common practice to hold agricultural fairs in conjunction with spring and fall religious festivals, and to these gatherings, cattle, dogs, and other livestock were brought for exchange. As time went on, it became customary to provide entertainment, too. Dogs often participated in such sporting events as bull baiting, bear baiting, and ratting. Then the dog that exhibited the greatest skill in the arena was also the one that brought the highest price when time came for barter or sale. Today, these fairs seem a far cry from our highly organized bench shows and field trials. But they were the forerunners of modern dog shows and played an important role in shaping the development of purebred dogs.

The first organized dog show was held at Newcastle, England, in 1859. Later that same year, a show was held at Birmingham. At both shows dogs were divided into four classes and only Pointers and Setters were entered. In 1860, the first dog show in Germany was held at Apoldo, where nearly one hundred dogs were exhibited and entries were divided into six groups. Interest expanded rapidly, and by the time the Paris Exhibition was held in 1878, the dog show was a fixture of international importance.

In the United States, the first organized bench show was held in 1874 in conjunction with the meeting of the Illinois State Sportsmen's Association in Chicago, and all entries were dogs of sporting breeds. Although the show was a rather casual affair, interest spread quickly. Before the end of the year, shows were held in Oswego, New York, Mineola, Long Island, and Memphis, Tennessee. And the latter combined a bench show with the first organized field trial ever held in the United States. In January 1875, an all-breed show (the first in the United States) was held at Detroit, Michigan. From then on, interest increased rapidly, though rules were not always uniform, for there was no organization through which to coordinate activities until September 1884

Benching area at Westminster Kennel Club Show.

Judging for Best in Show at Westminster Kennel Club Show.

when The American Kennel Club was founded. Now the largest dog registering organization in the world, the A.K.C. is an association of several hundred member clubs—all breed, specialty, field trial, and obedience groups—each represented by a delegate to the A.K.C. The several thousand shows and trials held annually in the United States do much to stimulate interest in breeding to produce better looking, sounder, purebred dogs. For breeders, shows provide a means of measuring the merits of their work as compared with accomplishments of other breeders. For hundreds of thousands of dog fanciers, they provide an absorbing hobby.

For both spectators and participating owners, field trials constitute a fascinating demonstration of dogs competing under actual hunting conditions, where emphasis is on excellence of performance. The trials are sponsored by clubs or associations of persons interested in hunting dogs. Trials for Pointing breeds, Dachshunds, Retrievers, Spaniels, and Beagles are under the jurisdiction of The American Kennel Club and information concerning such activities is published in "Pure Bred Dogs—American Kennel Gazette." Trials for Bird Dogs are run by rules and regulations of the Amateur Field Trial Clubs of America and information concerning them is published in "The American Field."

All purebred dogs of recognized breeds may be registered with The American Kennel Club and those of hunting breeds may also be registered with The American Field. Dogs that have won championships both in the field and in bench shows are known as dual champions.

At bench (or conformation) shows, dogs are rated comparatively on their physical qualities (or conformation) in accordance with breed Standards which have been approved by The American Kennel Club. Characteristics such as size, coat, color, placement of eye or ear, general soundness, etc., are the basis for selecting the best dog in a class. Only purebred dogs are eligible to compete and if the show is one where points toward a championship are to be awarded, a dog must be at least six months old.

Bench shows are of various types. An all-breed show has classes for all of the breeds recognized by The American Kennel Club as well as a Miscellaneous Class for breeds not recognized, such as the Australian Cattle Dog, the Ibizan Hound, the Spinoni Italiani, the Tibetan Terrier, etc. A sanctioned match is an informal meeting where dogs compete but not for championship points. A specialty show is confined to a single breed. Other shows may restrict entries to champions of record, to American-bred dogs, etc. Competition for Junior Showmanship or for Best Brace, Best Team, or Best Local Dog may be included. Also, obedience competition is held in conjunction with many bench shows.

The term "bench show" is somewhat confusing in that shows of this type may be either "benched" or "unbenched." At the former, each dog is assigned an individual numbered stall where he must remain throughout the show except for times when he is being judged, groomed, or exercised. At unbenched shows, no stalls are provided and dogs are kept in their owners' cars or in crates when not being judged.

A show where a dog is judged for conformation actually constitutes an elimination contest. To begin with, the dogs of a single breed compete with others of their breed in one of the regular classes: Puppy, Novice, Bred by Exhibitor, American-Bred, or Open, and, finally, Winners, where the top dogs of the preceding five classes meet. The next step is the judging for Best of Breed (or Best of Variety of Breed). Here the Winners Dog and Winners Bitch (or the dog named Winners if only one prize is awarded) compete with any champions that are entered, together with any undefeated dogs that have competed in additional non-regular classes. The dog named Best of Breed (or Best of Variety of Breed), then goes on to compete with the other Best of Breed winners in his Group. The dogs that win in Group competition then compete for the final and highest honor, Best in Show.

When the Winners Class is divided by sex, championship points are awarded the Winners Dog and Winners Bitch. If the Winners Class is not divided by sex, championship points are awarded the dog or bitch named Winners. The number of points awarded varies, depending upon such factors as the number of dogs competing, the Schedule of Points established by the Board of Directors of the A.K.C., and whether the dog goes on to win Best of Breed, the Group, and Best in Show.

In order to become a champion, a dog must win fifteen points, including points from at least two major wins—that is, at least two shows where three or more points are awarded. The major wins must be under two different judges, and one or more of the remaining points must be won under a third judge. The most points ever awarded at a show is five and the least is one, so, in order to become

**Junior Showmanship Competition at Westminster Kennel Club Show.**

a champion, a dog must be exhibited and win in at least three shows, and usually he is shown many times before he wins his championship.

"Pure Bred Dogs—American Kennel Gazette" and other dog magazines contain lists of forthcoming shows, together with names and addresses of sponsoring organizations to which you may write for entry forms and information relative to fees, closing dates, etc. Before entering your dog in a show for the first time, you should familiarize yourself with the regulations and rules governing competition. You may secure such information from The American Kennel Club or from a local dog club specializing in your breed. It is essential that you also familiarize yourself with the A.K.C. approved Standard for your breed so you will be fully aware of characteristics worthy of merit as well as those considered faulty, or possibly even serious enough to disqualify the dog from competition. For instance, monorchidism (failure of one testicle to descend) and cryptorchidism (failure of both testicles to descend) are disqualifying faults in all breeds.

If possible, you should first attend a show as a spectator and observe judging procedures from ringside. It will also be helpful to join a local breed club and to participate in sanctioned matches before entering an all-breed show.

The dog should be equipped with a narrow leather show lead and a show collar—never an ornamented or spiked collar. For benched shows, a metal-link bench chain will be needed to fasten the dog to the bench. For unbenched shows, the dog's crate should be taken along so that he may be confined in comfort when he is not appearing in the ring. A dog should never be left in a car with all the windows closed. In hot weather the temperature will become unbearable in a very short time. Heat exhaustion may result from even a short period of confinement, and death may ensue.

Food and water dishes will be needed, as well as a supply of the food and water to which the dog is accustomed. Brushes and combs are also necessary, so that you may give the dog's coat a final grooming after you arrive at the show.

Familiarize yourself with the schedule of classes ahead of time, for the dog must be fed and exercised and permitted to relieve himself, and any last-minute grooming completed before his class is called. Both you and the dog should be ready to enter the ring unhurriedly. A good deal of skill in conditioning, training, and handling is required if a dog is to be presented properly. And it is essential that the handler himself be composed, for a jittery handler will transmit his nervousness to his dog.

Once the class is assembled in the ring, the judge will ask that the dogs be paraded in line, moving counter-clockwise in a circle. If you have trained your dog well, you will have no difficulty controlling him in the ring, where he must change pace quickly and gracefully and walk and trot elegantly and proudly with head erect. The show dog must also stand quietly for inspection, posing like a statue for several minutes while the judge observes his structure in detail, examines teeth, feet, coat, etc. When the judge calls your dog forward for individual inspection, do not attempt to converse, but answer any questions he may ask.

As the judge examines the class, he measures each dog against the ideal described in the Standard, then measures the dogs against each other in a comparative sense and selects for first place the dog that comes closest to conforming to the Standard for its breed. If your dog isn't among the winners, don't grumble. If he places first, don't brag loudly. For a bad loser is disgusting, but a poor winner is insufferable.

## Obedience Competition

For hundreds of years, dogs have been used in England and Germany in connection with police and guard work, and their working potential has been evaluated through tests devised to show agility, strength, and courage. Organized training has also been popular with English and German breeders for many years, although it was first practiced primarily for the purpose of training large breeds in aggressive tactics.

There was little interest in obedience training in the United States until 1933 when Mrs. Whitehouse Walker returned from England and enthusiastically introduced the sport. Two years later, Mrs. Walker persuaded The American Kennel Club to approve organized obedience activities and to assume jurisdiction over obedience rules. Since then, interest has increased at a phenomenal rate, for obedience competition is not only a sport the average spectator can follow readily, but also a sport for which the average owner can train his own dog easily. Obedience competition is suitable for all breeds. Furthermore, there is no limit to the number of dogs that may win in competition, for each dog is scored individually on the basis of a point rating system.

The dog is judged on his response to certain commands, and if he gains a high enough score in three successive trials under different judges, he wins an obedience degree. Degrees awarded are "C.D."—Companion Dog; "C.D.X."—Companion Dog Excellent; and "U.D."—Utility Dog. A fourth degree, the "T.D.," or Tracking Dog degree, may be won at any time and tests for it are held apart from dog shows. The qualifying score is a minimum of 170 points out of a possible total of 200, with no score in any one exercise less than 50% of the points allotted.

Since obedience titles are progressive, earlier titles (with the exception of the tracking degree) are dropped as a dog acquires the next higher degree. If an obedience title is gained in another country in addition to the United States, that fact is signified by the word "International," followed by the title.

Trials for obedience trained dogs are held at most of the larger bench shows, and obedience training clubs are to be found in almost all communities today. Information concerning forthcoming trials and lists of obedience training clubs are included regularly in "Pure Bred Dogs—American Kennel Gazette"—and other dog magazines. Pamphlets containing rules and regulations governing obedience competition are available upon request from The American Kennel Club, 51 Madison Avenue, New York, N.Y. 10010. Rules are revised occasionally, so if you are interested in participating in obedience competition, you should be sure your copy of the regulations is current.

All dogs must comply with the same rules, although in broad jump, high jump, and bar jump competition, the jumps are adjusted to the size of the breed. Classes at obedience trials are divided into Novice (A and B), Open (A and B), and Utility (which may be divided into A and B, at the option of the sponsoring club and with the approval of The American Kennel Club).

The Novice class is for dogs that have not won the title Companion Dog. In Novice A, no person who has previously handled a dog that has won a C.D. title in the obedience ring at a licensed or member trial, and no person who has regularly trained such a dog, may enter or handle a dog. The handler must be the dog's owner or a member of the owner's immediate family. In Novice B, dogs may be handled by the owner or any other person.

The Open A class is for dogs that have won the C.D. title but have not won the C.D.X. title. Obedience judges and licensed handlers may not enter or handle dogs in this class. Each dog must be handled by the owner or by a member of his immediate family. The Open B class is for dogs that have won the title C.D. or C.D.X. A dog may continue to compete in this class after it has won the title U.D. Dogs in this class may be handled by the owner or any other person.

The Utility class is for dogs that have won the title C.D.X. Dogs that have won the title U.D. may continue to compete in this class, and dogs may be handled by the owner or any other person. Provided the A.K.C. approves, a club may choose to divide the Utility class into Utility A and Utility B. When this is done, the Utility A class is for dogs that have won the title C.D.X. and have not won the title U.D. Obedience judges and licensed handlers may not enter or handle dogs in this class. All other dogs that are eligible for the Utility class but not eligible for Utility A may be entered in Utility B.

Novice competition includes such exercises as heeling on and off lead, the stand for examination, coming on recall, and the long sit and the long down.

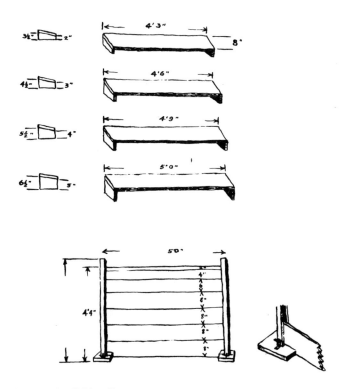

Broad jump and solid hurdle.

In Open competition, the dog must perform such exercises as heeling free, the drop on recall, and the retrieve on the flat and over the high jump. Also, he must execute the broad jump, and the long sit and long down.

In the Utility class, competition includes scent discrimination, the directed retrieve, the signal exercise, directed jumping, and the group examination.

Tracking is the most difficult test. It is always done out-of-doors, of course, and, for obvious reasons, cannot be held at a dog show. The dog must follow a scent trail that is about a quarter mile in length. He is also required to find a scent object (glove, wallet, or other article) left by a stranger who has walked the course to lay down the scent. The dog is required to follow the trail a half to two hours after the scent is laid.

An ideal way to train a dog for obedience competition is to join an obedience class or a training club. In organized class work, beginners' classes cover pretty much the same exercises as those

113

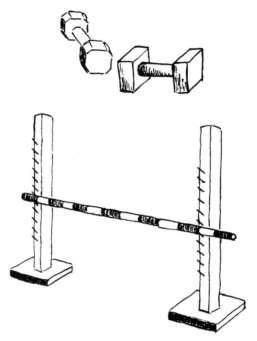

Dumbbells and bar jump.

described in the chapter on training. However, through class work you will develop greater precision than is possible in training your dog by yourself. Amateur handlers often cause the dog to be penalized, for if the handler fails to abide by the rules, it is the dog that suffers the penalty. A common infraction of the rules is using more than one signal or command where regulations stipulate only one may be used. Classwork will help eliminate such errors, which the owner may make unconsciously if he is working alone. Working with a class will also acquaint both dog and handler with ring procedure so that obedience trials will not present unforeseen problems.

Thirty or forty owners and dogs often comprise a class, and exercises are performed in unison, with individual instruction provided if it is required. The procedure followed in training—in fact, even wording of various commands—may vary from instructor to instructor. Equipment used will vary somewhat, also, but will usually include a training collar and leash such as those shown on page 109, a long line, a dumbbell, and a jumping stick.

The latter may be a short length of heavy doweling or a broom handle and both it and the dumbbell are usually painted white for increased visibility.

A bitch in season must never be taken to a training class, so before enrolling a female dog, you should determine whether she may be expected to come into season before classes are scheduled to end. If you think she will, it is better to wait and enroll her in a later course, rather than start the course and then miss classes for several weeks.

In addition to the time devoted to actual work in class, the dog must have regular, daily training sessions for practice at home. Before each class or home training session, the dog should be exercised so he will not be highly excited when the session starts, and he must be given an opportunity to relieve himself before the session begins. (Should he have an accident during the class, it is your responsibility to clean up after him.) The dog should be fed several hours before time for the class to begin or else after the class is over—never just before going to class.

If you decide to enter your dog in obedience competition, it is well to enter a small, informal show the first time. Dogs are usually called in the order in which their names appear in the catalog, so as soon as you arrive at the show, acquaint yourself with the schedule. If your dog is not the first to be judged, spend some time at ringside, observing the routine so you will know what to expect when your dog's turn comes.

In addition to collar, leash, and other equipment, you should take your dog's food and water pans and a supply of the food and water to which he is accustomed. You should also take his brushes and combs in order to give him a last-minute brushing before you enter the ring. It is important that the dog look his best even though he isn't to be judged on his appearance.

Before entering the ring, exercise your dog, give him a drink of water, and permit him to relieve himself. Once your dog enters the ring, give him your full attention and be sure to give voice commands distinctly so he will hear and understand, for there will be many distractions at ringside.

Top dogs in Utility Class. This illustrates variety of breeds that compete in obedience.

Genetics, the science of heredity, deals with the processes by which physical and mental traits of parents are transmitted to offspring. For centuries, man has been trying to solve these puzzles, but only in the last two hundred years has significant progress been made.

During the eighteenth century, Kölreuter, a German scientist, made revolutionary discoveries concerning plant sexuality and hybridization but was unable to explain just how hereditary processes worked. In the middle of the nineteenth century, Gregor Johann Mendel, an Augustinian monk, experimented with the ordinary garden pea and made other discoveries of major significance. He found that an inherited characteristic was inherited as a complete unit, and that certain characteristics predominated over others. Next, he observed that the hereditary characteristics of each parent are contained in each offspring, even when they are not visible, and that "hidden" characteristics can be transferred without change in their nature to the grandchildren, or even later generations. Finally, he concluded that although heredity contains an element of uncertainty, some things are predictable on the basis of well-defined mathematical laws.

Unfortunately, Mendel's published paper went unheeded, and when he died in 1884 he was still virtually unknown to the scientific world. But other researchers were making discoveries, too. In 1900, three different scientists reported to learned societies that much of their research in hereditary principles had been proved years before by Gregor Mendel and that findings matched perfectly.

Thus, hereditary traits were proved to be transmitted through the chromosomes found in pairs in every living being, one of each pair contributed by the mother, the other by the father. Within each chromosome have been found hundreds of smaller structures, or genes, which are the actual determinants of hereditary characteristics. Some genes are dominant and will be seen in the offspring. Others are recessive and will not be outwardly apparent, yet can be passed on to the offspring to combine with a similar recessive gene of the other parent and thus be seen. Or they may be passed on to the offspring, not be outwardly apparent, but be passed on again to become apparent in a later generation.

Once the genetic theory of inheritance became widely known, scientists began drawing a well-defined line between inheritance and environment. More recent studies show some overlapping of these influences and indicate a combination of the two may be responsible for certain characteristics. For instance, studies have proved that extreme cold increases the amount of black pigment in the skin and hair of the "Himalayan" rabbit, although it has little or no effect on the white or colored rabbit. Current research also indicates that even though characteristics are determined by the genes, some environmental stress occurring at a particular period of pregnancy might cause physical change in the embryo.

Long before breeders had any knowledge of genetics, they practiced one of its most important principles—selective breeding. Experience quickly showed that "like begets like," and by breeding like with like and discarding unlike offspring, the various individual breeds were developed to the point where variations were relatively few. Selective breeding is based on the idea of maintaining the quality of a breed at the highest possible level, while improving whatever defects are prevalent. It requires that only the top dogs in a litter be kept for later breeding, and that inferior specimens be ruthlessly eliminated.

In planning any breeding program, the first requisite is a definite goal—that is, to have clearly in mind a definite picture of the type of dog you wish eventually to produce. To attempt to breed perfection is to approach the problem unrealistically. But if you don't breed for improvement, it is preferable that you not breed at all.

As a first step, you should select a bitch that exemplifies as many of the desired characteristics as possible and mate her with a dog that also has as many of the desired characteristics as possible. If you start with mediocre pets, you will produce mediocre pet puppies. If you decide to start with more than one bitch, all should closely approach the type you desire, since you will

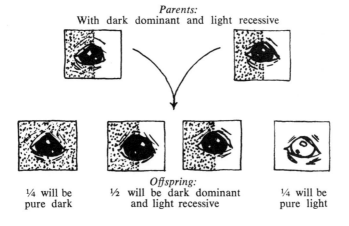

*Parents:*
One pure dark eyes
and one pure light eyes

Dark eyes        Light eyes

*Offspring:*
Eyes dark (dominant) with light recessive

*Parents:*
With dark dominant and light recessive

*Offspring:*

¼ will be
pure dark

½ will be dark dominant
and light recessive

¼ will be
pure light

The above is a schematic representation of the Mendelian law as it applies to the inheritance of eye color. The law applies in the same way to the inheritance of other physical characteristics.

then stand a better chance of producing uniformly good puppies from all. Breeders often start with a single bitch and keep the best bitches in every succeeding generation.

Experienced breeders look for "prepotency" in breeding stock —that is, the ability of a dog or bitch to transmit traits to most or all of its offspring. While the term is usually used to describe the transmission of good qualities, a dog may also be prepotent in transmitting faults. To be prepotent in a practical sense, a dog must possess many characteristics controlled by dominant genes. If desired characteristics are recessive, they will be apparent in the offspring only if carried by both sire and dam. Prepotent dogs and bitches usually come from a line of prepotent ancestors, but the mere fact that a dog has exceptional ancestors will not necessarily mean that he himself will produce exceptional offspring.

A single dog may sire a tremendous number of puppies, whereas a bitch can produce only a comparatively few litters during her lifetime. Thus, a sire's influence may be very widespread as compared to that of a bitch. But in evaluating a particular litter, it must be remembered that the bitch has had as much influence as has had the dog.

Inbreeding, line-breeding, outcrossing, or a combination of the three are the methods commonly used in selective breeding.

Inbreeding is the mating together of closely related animals, such as father-daughter, mother-son, or brother-sister. Although some breeders insist such breeding will lead to the production of defective individuals, it is through rigid inbreeding that all breeds of dogs have been established. Controlled tests have shown that any harmful effects appear within the first five or ten generations, and that if rigid selection is exercised from the beginning, a vigorous inbred strain will be built up.

Line-breeding is also the mating together of individuals related by family lines. However, matings are made not so much on the basis of the dog's and bitch's relationship to each other, but, instead, on the basis of their relationship to a highly admired ancestor, with a view to perpetuating his qualities. Line-breeding constitutes a long-range program and cannot be accomplished in a single generation.

Outcrossing is the breeding together of two dogs that are unrelated in family lines. Actually, since breeds have been developed through the mating of close relatives, all dogs within any given breed are related to some extent. There are few breedings that are true outcrosses, but if there is no common ancestor within five generations, a mating is usually considered an outcross.

Experienced breeders sometimes outcross for one generation in order to eliminate a particular fault, then go back to inbreeding or line-breeding. Neither the good effects nor the bad effects of outcrossing can be truly evaluated in a single mating, for undesirable recessive traits may be introduced into a strain, yet not show up for several generations. Outcrossing is better left to experienced breeders, for continual outcrossing results in a wide variation in type and great uncertainty as to the results that may be expected.

Two serious defects that are believed heritable—subluxation and orchidism—should be zealously guarded against, and afflicted dogs and their offspring should be eliminated from breeding programs. Subluxation is a condition of the hip joint where the bone of the socket is eroded and the head of the thigh bone is also worn away, causing lameness which becomes progressively more serious until the dog is unable to walk. Orchidism is the failure of one or both testicles to develop and descend properly. When one testicle is involved, the term "monorchid" is used. When both are involved, "cryptorchid" is used. A cryptorchid is almost always sterile, whereas a monorchid is usually fertile. There is evidence that orchidism "runs in families" and that a monorchid transmits the tendency through bitch and male puppies alike.

Through the years, many misconceptions concerning heredity have been perpetuated. Perhaps the one most widely perpetuated is the idea evolved hundreds of years ago that somehow characteristics were passed on through the mixing of the blood of the parents. We still use terminology evolved from that theory when we speak of bloodlines, or describe individuals as full-blooded, despite the fact that the theory was disproved more than a century ago.

Also inaccurate and misleading is any statement that a definite fraction or proportion of an animal's inherited characteristics can be positively attributed to a particular ancestor. Individuals lacking knowledge of genetics sometimes declare that an individual receives half his inherited characteristics from each parent, a quarter from each grandparent, an eighth from each great-grandparent, etc. Thousands of volumes of scientific findings have been published, but no simple way has been found to determine positively which characteristics have been inherited from which ancestors, for the science of heredity is infinitely complex.

Any breeder interested in starting a serious breeding program should study several of the excellent books on canine genetics that are currently available.

Whelping box. Detail at right shows proper side-wall construction which helps keep small puppies confined and provides sheltered nook which to prevent crushing or smothering.

## Breeding and Whelping

The breeding life of a bitch begins when she comes into season the first time at the age of about one to two years (depending on what breed she is). Thereafter, she will come in season at roughly six-month intervals, but this, too, is subject to variation. Her maximum fertility builds up from puberty to full maturity and then declines until a state of total sterility is reached in old age. Just when this occurs is hard to determine, for the fact that an older bitch shows signs of being in season doesn't necessarily mean she is still capable of reproducing.

The length of the season varies from eighteen to twenty-one days. The first indication is a pronounced swelling of the vulva with coincidental bleeding (called "showing color") for about the first seven to nine days. The discharge gradually turns to a creamy color, and it is during this phase (estrus), from about the tenth to the fifteenth days, that the bitch is ovulating and is receptive to the male. The ripe, unfertilized ova survive for about seventy-two hours. If fertilization doesn't occur, the ova die and are discharged the next time the bitch comes in season. If fertilization does take place, each ovum attaches itself to the walls of the uterus, a membrane forms to seal it off, and a foetus develops from it.

Following the estrus phase, the bitch is still in season until about the twenty-first day and will continue to be attractive to males, although she will usually fight them off as she did the first few days. Nevertheless, to avoid accidental mating, the bitch must be confined for the entire period. Virtual imprisonment is necessary, for male dogs display uncanny abilities in their efforts to reach a bitch in season.

The odor that attracts the males is present in the bitch's urine, so it is advisable to take her a good distance from the house before permitting her to relieve herself. To eliminate problems completely, your veterinarian can prescribe a preparation that will disguise the odor but will not interfere with breeding when the time is right. Many fanciers use such preparations when exhibiting a bitch and find that nearby males show no interest whatsoever. But it is not advisable to permit a bitch to run loose when she has been given a product of this type, for during estrus she will seek the company of male dogs and an accidental mating may occur.

A potential brood bitch, regardless of breed, should have good bone, ample breadth and depth of ribbing, and adequate room in the pelvic region. Unless a bitch is physically mature—well beyond the puppy stage when she has her first season—breeding should be delayed until her second or a later season. Furthermore, even though it is possible for a bitch to conceive twice a year, she should not be bred oftener than once a year. A bitch that is bred too often will age prematurely and her puppies are likely to lack vigor.

Two or three months before a bitch is to be mated, her physical condition should be considered carefully. If she is too thin, provide a rich, balanced diet plus the regular exercise needed to develop strong, supple muscles. Daily exercise on the lead is as necessary for the too-thin bitch as for the too fat one, although the latter will need more exercise and at a brisker pace, as well as a reduction of food, if she is to be brought to optimum condition. A prospective brood bitch must have had permanent distemper shots as well as rabies vaccination. And a month before her season is due, a veterinarian should examine a stool specimen for worms. If there is evidence of infestation, the bitch should be wormed.

A dog may be used at stud from the time he reaches physical maturity, well on into old age. The first time your bitch is bred, it is well to use a stud that has already proven his ability by having sired other litters. The fact that a neighbor's dog is readily available should not influence your choice, for to produce the best puppies, you must select the stud most suitable from a genetic standpoint.

If the stud you prefer is not going to be available at the time your bitch is to be in season, you may wish to consult your veterinarian concerning medications available for inhibiting the onset of the season. With such preparations, the bitch's season can be delayed indefinitely.

Usually the first service will be successful. However, if it isn't, in most cases an additional service is given free, provided the stud dog is still in the possession of the same owner. If the bitch misses, it may be because her cycle varies widely from normal. Through microscopic examination, a veterinarian can determine exactly when the bitch is entering the estrus phase and thus is likely to conceive.

The owner of the stud should give you a stud-service certificate, providing a four-generation pedigree for the sire and showing the date of mating. The litter registration application is completed only after the puppies are whelped, but it, too, must be signed by the owner of the stud as well as the owner of the bitch. Registration forms may be secured by writing The American Kennel Club.

In normal pregnancy there is usually visible enlargement of the abdomen by the end of the fifth week. By palpation (feeling with the fingers) a veterinarian may be able to distinguish developing puppies as early as three weeks after mating, but it is unwise for a novice to poke and prod, and try to detect the presence of unborn puppies.

The gestation period normally lasts nine weeks, although it may vary from sixty-one to sixty-five days. If it goes beyond sixty-five days from the date of mating, a veterinarian should be consulted.

During the first four or five weeks, the bitch should be permitted her normal amount of activity. As she becomes heavier, she should be walked on the lead, but strenuous running and jumping should be avoided. Her diet should be well balanced (see page 43), and if she should become constipated, small amounts of mineral oil may be added to her food.

A whelping box should be secured about two weeks before the puppies are due, and the bitch should start then to use it as her bed so she will be accustomed to it by the time puppies arrive. Preferably, the box should be square, with each side long enough so that the bitch can stretch out full length and have several inches to spare at either end. The bottom should be padded with an old cotton rug or other material that is easily laundered. Edges of the padding should be tacked to the floor of the box so the puppies will not get caught in it and smother. Once it is obvious labor is about to begin, the padding should be covered with several layers of spread-out newspapers. Then, as papers become soiled, the top layer can be pulled off, leaving the area clean.

Forty-eight to seventy-two hours before the litter is to be whelped, a definite change in the shape of the abdomen will be noted. Instead of looking barrel-shaped, the abdomen will sag pendulously. Breasts usually redden and become enlarged, and milk may be present a day or two before the puppies are whelped. As the time becomes imminent, the bitch will probably scratch and root at her bedding in an effort to make a nest, and will refuse food and ask to be let out every few minutes. But the surest sign is a drop in temperature of two or three degrees about twelve hours before labor begins.

The bitch's abdomen and flanks will contract sharply when labor actually starts, and for a few minutes she will attempt to expel a puppy, then rest for a while and try again. Someone should stay with the bitch the entire time whelping is taking place, and if she appears to be having unusual difficulties, a veterinarian should be called.

Puppies are usually born head first, though some may be born feet first and no difficulty encountered. Each puppy is enclosed in a separate membranous sac that the bitch will remove with her teeth. She will sever the umbilical cord, which will be attached to the soft, spongy afterbirth that is expelled right after the puppy emerges. Usually the bitch eats the afterbirth, so it is necessary to watch and make sure one is expelled for each puppy whelped. If afterbirth is retained, the bitch may develop peritonitis and die.

The dam will lick and nuzzle each newborn puppy until it is warm and dry and ready to nurse. If puppies arrive so close together that she can't take care of them, you can help her by rubbing the puppies dry with a soft .cloth. If several have been whelped but the bitch continues to be in labor, all but one should be removed and placed in a small box lined with clean towels and warmed to about seventy degrees. The bitch will be calmer if one puppy is left with her at all times.

Whelping sometimes continues as long as twenty-four hours for a very large litter, but a litter of two or three puppies may be whelped in an hour. When the bitch settles down, curls around the puppies and nuzzles them to her, it usually indicates that all have been whelped.

The bitch should be taken away for a few minutes while you clean the box and arrange clean padding. If her coat is soiled, sponge it clean before she returns to the puppies. Once she is back in the box, offer her a bowl of warm beef broth and a pan of cool water, placing both where she will not have to get up in order to reach them. As soon as she indicates interest in food, give her a generous bowl of chopped meat to which codliver oil and dicalcium phosphate have been added (see page 43).

If inadequate amounts of calcium are provided during the period the puppies are nursing, eclampsia may develop. Symptoms are violent trembling, rapid rise in temperature, and rigidity of muscles. Veterinary assistance must be secured immediately, for death may result in a very short time. Treatment consists of massive doses of calcium gluconate administered intravenously, after which symptoms subside in a miraculously short time.

All puppies are born blind and their eyes open when they are ten to fourteen days old. At first the eyes have a bluish cast and appear weak, and the puppies must be protected from strong light until at least ten days after the eyes open.

To ensure proper emotional development, young dogs should be shielded from loud noises and rough handling. Being lifted by the front legs is painful and may result in permanent injury to the shoulders. So when lifting a puppy, always place one hand under the chest with the forefinger between the front legs, and place the other hand under his bottom.

Sometimes the puppies' nails are so long and sharp that they scratch the bitch's breasts. Since the nails are soft, they can be trimmed with ordinary scissors.

If of a breed that ordinarily has a docked tail, puppies should have their tails shortened when they are three days old. Dew-claws—thumblike appendages appearing on the inside of the legs of some breeds—are removed at the same time. While both are simple procedures, they shouldn't be attempted by amateurs.

In certain breeds it is customary to crop the ears, also. This should be done at about eight weeks of age. Cropping should never be attempted by anyone other than a veterinarian, for it requires use of anesthesia and knowledge of surgical techniques, as well as judgment as to the eventual size of the dog and proportion of ear to be removed so the head will be balanced when the dog is mature.

At about four weeks of age, formula should be provided. The amount fed each day should be increased over a period of two weeks, when the puppies can be weaned completely. The formula should be prepared as described on page 41, warmed to luke-warm, and poured into a shallow pan placed on the floor of the box. After his mouth has been dipped into the mixture a few times, a puppy will usually start to lap formula. All puppies should be allowed to eat from the same pan, but be sure the small ones get their share. If they are pushed aside, feed them separately. Permit the puppies to nurse part of the time, but gradually increase the number of meals of formula. By the time the puppies are five weeks old, the dam should be allowed with them only at night. When they are about six weeks old, they should be weaned completely and fed the puppy diet described on page 41.

Once they are weaned, puppies should be given temporary distemper injections every two weeks until they are old enough for permanent inoculations. At six weeks, stool specimens should be checked for worms, for almost without exception, puppies become infested. Specimens should be checked again at eight weeks, and as often thereafter as your veterinarian recommends.

Sometimes owners decide as a matter of convenience to have a bitch spayed or a male castrated. While this is recommended when a dog has a serious inheritable defect or when abnormalities of reproductive organs develop, in sound, normal purebred dogs, spaying a bitch or castrating a male may prove a definite disadvantage. The operations automatically bar dogs from competing in shows as well as precluding use for breeding. The operations are seldom dangerous, but they should not be performed without good reason.